OVERCOMING
THE WORLD

OVERCOMING
THE WORLD

GRACE TO WIN
THE DAILY BATTLE

JOEL R. BEEKE

PUBLISHING
P.O. BOX 817 • PHILLIPSBURG • NEW JERSEY 08865-0817

Scripture quotations are from the The Holy Bible, King James Version.

Italics within Scripture quotations indicate emphasis added.

Page design and typesetting by Lakeside Design Plus

Printed in the United States of America

Library of Congress Cataloging-in-Publication Data

Beeke, Joel R., 1952–
    Overcoming the world : grace to win the daily battle / Joel R. Beeke.
        p. cm.
    Includes bibliographical references and index.
    ISBN 0-87552-746-9
    1. Christian life—Reformed authors. 2. Worldliness. I. Title.

BV4501.3.B435 2005
248.4'842—dc22

                                                                2004060125

CONTENTS

PREFACE

Worldliness is destroying the church of Jesus Christ. Christians and churches that fall prey to it lose their saltiness. The time is thus right for us to biblically expose and condemn worldliness, and to promote the alternatives of genuine piety and holiness.

This book addresses this need from a practical perspective. Its chapters enlarge upon four addresses given at the Metropolitan Tabernacle School of Theology in London on July 2–4, 2002. The first address, a sermon on 1 John 5:4–5 (chs. 1–3), shows how worldliness can be overcome only by saving faith in Jesus Christ. The second address shows how Calvin's view of piety forms a comprehensive, positive answer to the problem of worldliness—theologically, ecclesiastically, and personally (chs. 4–7). The third address calls us to cultivate holiness as an antidote to worldliness (chs. 8–12). The last address, based on Acts 20:28, examines how ministers and others serving the Lord can overcome worldliness (chs. 13–22). The second and third addresses are revisions of material printed in *The Cambridge Companion to John Calvin*, edited by Donald McKim (Cambridge: University Press, 2004), 125–52; "Cultivating Holiness," *Reformation & Revival* 4.2 (Spring 1995): 81–112; and *Holiness: God's Call to Sanctification* (Edinburgh: Banner of Truth Trust, 1994).

I thank Dr. Peter and Jill Masters for their hospitality and friendship, and for repeatedly inviting me to serve the historic Metropolitan Tabernacle. Thanks, too, to the helpful staff at the Tabernacle. What a joy it is to speak at the Met Tab School of Theology! We pray that God's rich blessing may rest upon both church and school, and that this book may help turn many from worldly ways to the path of genuine Reformed piety and holiness.

Hearty thanks to my dear wife Mary, God's humbling gift to me, to my children (Calvin, Esther, and Lydia), and to the Heritage Netherlands Reformed Congregation and the Puritan Reformed Theological Seminary for granting me the time to absent myself from my regular round of duties to serve at the Tabernacle.

PART 1

OVERCOMING
THE
WORLD
BY
FAITH

WHAT IS OVERCOMING WORLDLINESS?

The most valuable things in life are not easily obtained, much less retained. That is true of the spiritual blessing of a personal saving relationship with God, of an intimate biblical marriage, of close ties with family and friends, of divine approval of our work, of contentment in Christ, and of a disciplined lifestyle of commitment to His church and kingdom.

None of these blessings should be taken for granted. In spiritual life, in interpersonal relations, in all of our work, this principle holds true: the path to gain is through pain.

In their book *In His Image*, Paul Brand and Philip Yancey show how pain is a necessary ingredient to growth.[1] That's why we speak of growing pains and repeat the saying "No pain, no gain." In nature, struggle and pain are also necessary for proper growth. Consider as an example the story of a man who once found a cocoon of the emperor moth and took it home to watch it emerge. One day a small opening appeared. For several hours the moth struggled but couldn't seem to force its body past a certain point. Deciding something was wrong, the man took scissors and snipped the remaining bit of cocoon. The moth emerged easily, its body large and swollen, the wings small and shriveled. The man expected that in a few hours the wings of the moth would unfurl in their natural beauty, but they did not. The moth spent its life dragging around a swollen body and shriveled wings. The struggle and pain necessary to pass through the tiny opening of the cocoon are God's way of forcing fluid from the body of a moth into the wings. The merciful snip of the scissors was, in reality, most cruel.

Likewise, the Christian life is a struggle. It demands entrance through a narrow gate and a daily walk along a narrow path. The Christian way is not a middle way between extremes but a narrow way between precipices. It involves living by faith through self-denial, waging a holy war in the midst of a hostile world. And what a war it is, for the world doesn't fight fairly or clearly, doesn't agree to ceasefires, and doesn't sign peace treaties.

To see how the believer can overcome the way of worldliness, let's examine 1 John 5:4–5, which says, "For whatsoever is born of God overcometh the world: and this is the victory that overcometh the world, even our faith. Who is he that overcometh the world, but he that believeth that Jesus is the Son of God?" With God's help, we shall look at overcoming worldliness by faith in three parts: what it means (ch. 1), how it is practiced (ch. 2), and how to make it last (ch. 3).

Earlier in his epistle John encourages us to flee worldliness. First John 2:15–17 says, "Love not the world, neither the things that are in the world. If any man love the world, the love of the Father is not in him. For all that is in the world, the lust of the flesh, and the lust of the eyes, and the pride of life, is not of the Father, but is of the world. And the world passeth away, and the lust thereof: but he that doeth the will of God abideth for ever."

Here John contrasts love for the world with love for the Father. The two loves are incompatible. As Jesus said, "No man can serve two masters: for either he will hate the one, and love the other; or else he will hold to the one, and despise the other" (Matt. 6:24). One love must rule our lives: a holy passion for God and the things of God. The choice is clear and the directions simple, but the way is not easy. As Jesus said, "Watch and pray, that ye enter not into temptation: the spirit indeed is willing, but the flesh is weak" (Matt. 26:41).

What does John mean by the "world"? The Greek word *kosmos*, or "world," has several meanings in the New Testament. In 1 John 5:4 the apostle does not refer to the physical world in which we live or to the mass of people living on the planet. Rather, he uses the term to refer to a kingdom of which the ruler and the inhabitants are lost in sin and wholly at odds with anything pleasing to God. John is talking about Satan's kingdom of darkness, which includes all people who are under his rule and living according to the standards of this world.

In our text, "world" is a realm in opposition to Christ and His church. This world, though created to reflect the glory of God, now lives in rebellion against the Lord and His Christ (Ps. 2:2). It has become a fallen, disordered world in the grip of the evil one, rebellious, and alienated because of Adam's broken relationship with God. The world is sinful mankind *en masse*, under the god of this world (2 Cor. 4:4), given to unrighteousness, hostile to the truth and to the people of God. It is men, women, and children who focus on this world's lusts and neglect the world to come. Despite its great achievements, this world is lost and incapable of saving itself.[2]

15

The goal of worldly people is to move forward rather than upward, to live horizontally rather than vertically. They seek after outward prosperity rather than holiness. They burst with selfish desires rather than heartfelt supplications. If they do not deny God, they ignore and forget Him, or else they use Him only for their selfish ends.

Worldliness, then, is human nature without God. Someone who is of this world is controlled by worldly pursuits: the quest for pleasure, profit, and position. A worldly man yields to the spirit of fallen mankind—the spirit of self-seeking and self-indulgence—without regard for God. Each one of us, by nature, was born worldly. We belong to this evil world; it is our natural habitat.

By nature, we have a worldly mind that is "not subject to the law of God, neither indeed can be" (Rom. 8:7). As much as we were nourished by an umbilical cord in our mother's womb, so we were tied to the world from birth. Our understanding has been darkened (Eph. 4:18) by the guilt of Adam's sin, which was passed on to us. Despite our natural worldliness, John speaks, quite astonishingly, of overcoming that liability. He says, "For whatsoever is born of God overcometh the world." John uses that phrase sixteen times in his writings—more than all the rest of the Bible writers put together. But what exactly does he mean by "overcoming the world"?

John does not mean conquering the people of this world, winning power battles over our colleagues, or dominating others. He isn't referring to rulers such as Alexander the Great, who, after conquering the world, regretted that he had no more worlds to conquer.

Nor does John mean withdrawing from the world, such as monks or Amish people tend to do by establishing their own communities. A Christian is called to fight *in* this world even though he is not *of* this world. He must live in the world but not let the world live in him. Escaping is not overcoming. To escape from the world is like a soldier avoiding injury by running from the battlefield. Spiritual conscientious objectors have no place in the kingdom of God, for Christians are called to a war, not invited to a picnic.

Overcoming also doesn't mean sanctifying everything in the world for Christ. Some parts of the world may be redeemed for Christ, but sinful activities can never be sanctified. We don't need to Christianize drama or dance for public worship, for example, or try to Christianize what Hollywood has to offer by way of entertainment.

For John, overcoming means fighting by faith against the flow of this present evil world. Overcoming the world entails several essential aspects: (1) a decision to overcome worldliness; (2) freedom and perseverance through Christ; (3) rising above worldly circumstances; and (4) a life of self-denial.

A Decision to Overcome Worldliness

Someone who wants to overcome the world realizes that he has something to overcome. He sees that he has been floating with this world's mentality—thinking the way this world thinks, speaking the way this world speaks, and spending time and energy in the pursuit of worldly things. He now realizes that his thoughts, words, and actions have all been worldly—that he has done nothing to the glory of God or out of true faith in obedience to the spirit of God's law. "I have wasted my life," he cries out. "Rather than overcoming this world, I have been overcome by this world. Its selfishness, pride, and materialism have swallowed me up."

Someone who overcomes the world makes a clean break from worldly friends, worldly activities, and worldly habits. Like Joshua he decides, "As for me and my house, we will serve the LORD" (Josh. 24:15). He takes the cold plunge into potential rejection by the world, placing the fear of God above the fear of man, and esteeming God's desires of greater value than the desires of men.

Freedom and Perseverance through Christ

Perseverance against worldliness takes great grace, for the battle is intense (see Rom. 7). Worldly temptations entice us. Worldly people beguile us. Internal worldliness afflicts us. Satan, ruler of this world, knows our weaknesses. At times the attacks may be so powerful that we cry out with Paul, "O wretched man that I am! who shall deliver me from the body of this death?" (v. 24).

By grace, one who would overcome the world strives for allegiance to God rather than the world. Finding freedom only in Christ and His service, he cries out, "Lord, Thou hast loosed my bonds; I will fight against returning to the slavery of sin with all that is within me." He sings with all his heart:

> I am, O Lord, Thy servant, bound yet free,
> Thy handmaid's son, whose shackles Thou hast
> broken;
> Redeemed by grace, I'll render as a token
> Of gratitude my constant praise to Thee.
> —Psalter 426 (Psalm 116), stanza 9[3]

Rising above the Circumstances of This World

Paul learned to be content in whatever state he found himself (Phil. 4:11). Neither poverty nor wealth nor sorrow nor joy could move Paul from Christ-centered living. That's what it means to overcome the world—to live, for Christ's sake, above the threats and bribes and jokes of the world. It means following the Lord like Caleb (Num. 14:24) in the midst of complainers. It means remaining at peace when friends or people at work despise us for serving the Lord. It means patiently enduring all the persecutions the world throws at us.

Dr. Peter Hammond, whom I met in South Africa, told me that every time he preaches in Sudan, he expects to be arrested and persecuted. When pressed for details on how he was persecuted, Dr. Hammond said he had experienced "minor persecution," such as having his head submerged in a pail of urine until he was forced to drink it, or having a bag tied around his head at the neck until he fainted from lack of oxygen. "That's nothing compared to what our Lord experienced," he quickly added. "We Christians must count it all joy when we are persecuted for Christ's sake."

Most of us do not suffer such persecution, but if we are to overcome the world, we must not expect to be friends of this world. As John tells us, worldly people who hate Christ will also hate His disciples. Luther said that suffering persecution is an inevitable mark of being a believer. If you are a true Christian, expect persecution. Second Timothy 3:12 says, "All that will live godly in Christ Jesus shall suffer persecution." Remember that a world that smiles upon you is a dangerous place.

Pray for grace to resist worldly temptation. Strive to follow Spurgeon's advice: "Overcome the world by patiently enduring all the persecution that falls to your lot. Do not get angry; and do not become downhearted. Jests break no bones; and if you had any bone broken for Christ's sake, it would be the most honored bone in your whole body."[4]

Living a Life of Self-Denial

Abraham is a prime example of self-denial. When God called him to leave his family and friends in Haran, Abraham obeyed, not knowing where he was going. When the well-watered plain of Jordan lay before him, he didn't ask to move there, as his nephew Lot did. When Lot was carried off into captivity, Abraham fought to free him, then refused to take anything from the defeated kings, though he had every right to the spoils of war according to the customs of his day.

Abraham also denied himself in the supreme test of his faith in God. When God commanded him to sacrifice his son Isaac, through whom all the promises of the covenant would come, Abraham rose up early, unsheathed his knife, and prepared to offer his son in obedience to God.[5] May God grant us such self-denying devotion, for that is what it takes to overcome the world.

2

PRACTICING THE OVERCOMING LIFE

y nature, we don't possess the faith of Abraham. We are dead in our sins (Eph. 2:1–2) until God graciously makes us His own (John 3:5). Only then are we called out of this sinful world to become living members of the kingdom of God. As John tells us, "Whatsoever is born of God overcometh the world" (1 John 5:4).

To be born of God is to be regenerated. Regeneration is that secret act of God by which He gives new life to a sinner and makes the governing disposition of his soul holy. Regeneration is not merely reformation, religion, or education, as Nicodemus discovered in his talk with Jesus (John 3). Rather, it is resurrection from the dead and a re-creation (Eph. 2:1; 2 Cor. 4:16) that God miraculously works within us. As John Stott said, "It is a supernatural event which takes us out of the sphere of the world where Satan rules, and into the family of God. The spell of the old life has been broken; the fascination of the world has lost its appeal."[1]

Those reborn of God have such a radical change of heart that they become new creatures with radically different views of sin, the world, Christ, and Scripture. They hate sin and long to flee from it. They hate what they used to love, and love what they used to hate. They long to know Christ and to live to please Him. Such people, John says, "overcome the world." In this respect, this overcoming is a completed and once-for-all act. Everyone born of God *has* overcome the world, John says.

Objectively, this act took place when the Son of God lived, died, and rose from the dead, thus triumphing over sin and hell. Jesus Christ defeated Satan and the world on behalf of all those given to Him by the Father from eternity. Subjectively, this act takes place in the lives of sinners who are made partakers of Christ's great act of atonement through regeneration. In John 15:19 Jesus said, "Ye are not of the world, but I have chosen you out of the world." Because of Christ's death, God's people have been plucked from the kingdom of this world and given to Christ and the kingdom of heaven. Through Jesus Christ they have now overcome the world, the flesh, and the devil. As 1 John 2:13 says, "I write unto you, young men, because ye have overcome the wicked one."

We are victors because we belong to the Victor. What a great thing to realize as we find ourselves at war with this world. We are victors, not because we are great warriors, but because we belong to the One who has triumphed.

Overcoming the world is still a daily battle, however. John reminds us of that in 1 John 5:5, when he says, "Who is he that overcometh the world, but he that believeth that Jesus is the Son of God?" Here John uses the present tense to focus on how this overcoming continues to occur in the present. We have overcome the world because we belong to the One who has overcome, but we also must strive to win daily battles against the world. By the grace of the Holy Spirit, here's how we are to do that.

When a person is born again, he begins to overcome the world. The Christian is still attracted to the world because of the sin that remains in him, however. The Bible calls this remaining attraction "the flesh." Thus, while we must keep ourselves "unspotted from the world," as James 1:27 says, we must remember that our "flesh" is still inclined toward the world. That is why isolation from the world cannot keep us from sin. We who are believers carry a piece of the world within us.

No nature but the divine nature will try to overcome the world. Believers, by grace, have that nature. They are, as Peter says, "partakers of the divine nature" (2 Peter 1:4). The Holy Spirit is in them. They are united with Christ Jesus. And they are adopted by the Father. By the grace of God they can overcome the world. As 1 John 5:4 says, "For whatsoever is born of God overcometh the world: and this is the victory that overcometh the world, even our faith." In Christ, we have overcome the world, but we must also daily fight against the temptations of the world. That can only be done by faith.

In 1 John 2:16, John names three ways in which we are lured into the ways of the world: the lust of the flesh, the lust of the eyes, and the pride of life. In Christ's strength, faith battles against these paths of worldliness in order to overcome the world.

Lust of the Flesh

First, faith battles against the *lust of the flesh*. Faith refuses to love a world that delights in the lusts of the flesh. That means resisting temptations, such as illicit drugs, smoking, overeating, or excessive drinking. The Bible repeatedly warns against such excesses. We must not be brought under bondage to anything physical but are to exercise self-control, for our body is the temple of the Holy Ghost (1 Cor. 6:12; 9:27; 3:17).

The prohibition against fleshly lusting forbids sexual immorality in all forms. It forbids any flirtation or physical intimacy outside of marriage. God has wisely placed sexual intimacy within the sanctity of marriage.

We must also be modest about the way we dress, so that it does not encourage lust. Clothing that calls attention to our bodies arouses fleshly lusts that offend God. He blames those who provoke lust as much as those who lust after them.

Refusing to love the world means keeping ourselves and our children from worldly music, worldly parties, unedifying entertainment, night clubs, and all that stirs the lusts of the flesh. We must ask of all forms of entertainment: Can I pray over this? Does it glorify God or ignite fleshly lusts? Does it pass the test of Philippians 4:8, being "honest, just, pure, lovely, and of good report"?

Each of us must strive to know our own heart and its weaknesses to particular lusts. In *Not Even a Hint,* Joshua Harris has powerfully shown that we must avoid as much as possible whatever encourages particular lusts in us, even when what we should avoid may appear lawful in itself.[2]

Faith refuses to love this present evil world. Rather, it heeds Romans 13:14, which says, "Put ye on the Lord Jesus Christ, and make not provision for the flesh, to fulfil the lusts thereof."

Lust of the Eyes

Second, faith battles against the *lust of the eyes*. Satan works very hard to engage our eyes in worldly entertainment. Just as he tempted our first parents to believe that their Creator was hard and unbending, so he whispers to us, "When did God say that you couldn't enjoy movies or television shows that repeatedly break His commandments? Doesn't He want you to know what's going on in the world? Only a hard, legalistic God would deny those to you."

Satan has been using such arguments since paradise. He knows his time is short, so he will do anything to persuade us to look at the temptations of worldly entertainment. Perhaps he'll even use a friend to entice us, as he used Eve to tempt Adam. Satan is a master at hiding himself under the cloak of friendship.

Today Satan makes such fruit even more tempting by allowing us to see it in the privacy of our home—in videos or over the Internet. We must say no to all forms of entertainment which teach that man is in control of his world and that glamorize sin. Such entertainment makes adultery look innocent, commonplace, or even exciting. Murder becomes thrilling. Profanity is everyday speech. We cannot trust our own strength in this, for even the apostle Paul admitted, "For I know that in me (that is, in my flesh,) dwelleth no good thing: for to will is present with me; but how to perform that which is good I find not. For the good that I would I do not: but the evil which I would not, that I do" (Rom. 7:18–19).

Let us also rid our homes of unedifying magazines, trashy novels, indeed, all printed material that contradicts the Ten Commandments. How can we ask not to be led into temptation while we continue to play with temptation? As James warns us, "Every man is tempted, when he is drawn away of his own lust, and enticed. Then when lust hath conceived, it bringeth forth sin: and sin, when it is finished, bringeth forth death" (James 1:14–15).

Flee the lusts of the eyes. Practice self-denial. Follow Paul, who said, "Herein do I exercise myself, to have always a conscience void of offense toward God, and toward men" (Acts 24:16).

Pride of Life

Finally, faith battles against *the pride of life*. How prevalent such pride is in our hearts. As George Swinnock said, "Pride is the shirt of the soul put on first and put off last."[3] The pride of life includes:

- *Pride in ourselves and our accomplishments.* By nature we are filled with a desire for self-gratification and self-fulfillment. We live for ourselves, promoting our own wisdom and accomplishments.
- *Pride in challenging the providential governing of God.* Sects such as Mormonism and Jehovah's Witnesses challenge God's rule by asserting man's power to save himself by his own efforts. So do the New Age Movement, transcendental meditation, and occult practices such as fortune-telling, horoscopes, ouija boards, and palm-reading. So do attempts to manipulate and destroy life through artificial birth control, abortion, or euthanasia, all of which intrude upon and usurp the role of divine providence.
- *Pride in idolizing* movie actors, sports heroes, government leaders, or other popular figures. John condemns all human idolization as the pride of life.
- *Pride of materialism.* Loving possessions such as our homes or cars or clothing more than God is idolatrous as it feeds our quest for pleasure. Dishonesty in business, tax evasion, and other unethical ways of increasing personal wealth feed the pride of life; so does envy or the wish to become rich at the expense of our spir-

itual welfare. Pride of life involves gambling and lot-
teries, and everything that prohibits our first fruits from
being given to the Lord.

• *Pride of desecrating the Lord's Day.* How proud we
must be to think that we don't need to set aside one
day out of seven to worship the Lord and to receive the
kind of spiritual food that will nurture us for the coming week.

Faith strives against these paths of worldliness. It helps us
gain victory over all the subtle power of external and internal
worldliness in a variety of ways:

1. Believing in Jesus the Son of God. John asks, "Who is he that
overcometh the world, but he that believeth that Jesus is the Son
of God?" (1 John 5:5). When we become believers, we have a new
nature that is different from the world. Our minds are enlightened, our consciences quickened, and our hearts stirred. In practice, this works through faith. By faith we believe that Jesus is the
Son of God and overcome the world by looking away from ourselves and our weakness to His strength.

After writing about the conflicts endured by biblical heroes
of faith, the writer of Hebrews says the only way these people
endured stonings, burnings, drownings, tortures, and other
persecutions was by "looking unto Jesus the author and fin-
isher of our faith; who for the joy that was set before him
endured the cross, despising the shame, and is set down at the
right hand of the throne of God" (Heb. 12:2).

If we would overcome the world, we must look by faith to
Jesus, the Son of God, who endured the cross. The cross spelled
victory for Christ, for it meant crushing the head of the ser-
pent (Gen. 3:15) and finishing the work of suffering that His
Father gave Him to do (John 19:30). Jesus chose to be nailed
on the cross rather than be crowned king of the world. And in

those dreadful hours on the cross, the world was vanquished at His feet.

Jesus' victory on the cross was for you, dear believer. The cross is also your way to glory. When you are faced with worldly temptation, ask yourself, "Shall I do this great wickedness against my Savior, and sin against His cross?" Then confess with Paul, "God forbid that I should glory, save in the cross of our Lord Jesus Christ, by whom the world is crucified unto me, and I unto the world" (Gal. 6:14). Sing with Isaac Watts:

> Forbid it, Lord, that I should boast,
> Save in the death of Christ, my God;
> All the vain things that charm me most,
> I sacrifice them to His blood.

You must also look to Jesus the Son of God as Almighty Intercessor and Advocate, very God of very God, if you would overcome the world. As Paul says, "In him dwelleth all the fulness of the Godhead bodily" (Col. 2:9). Everything you need in your battle against the principalities and powers of the world is to be found in Christ. You are more than a conqueror through the One who loved you so much that He died for you.

Faith obtains victory over the powers of this world because faith enables us to draw upon the resources of Christ. If you want your lamp to work, you must connect it with a power source. Likewise, faith connects us to the mighty resources of the One who has overcome the world. Those resources include Christ's merit, His life, His Spirit, and His graces.

Faith in Christ overcomes the world by reconciling us with God via the cross and delivering us from the kingdom of Satan. It makes us feel at home with God and His kingdom rather than with the devil and this world. It gives us new affections through the Holy Spirit. We can truly say with Paul, "For to me to live is Christ" (Phil. 1:21). Trusting in Christ alone is so simple and yet so difficult. Such faith relies utterly upon the power of His might. No wonder Matthew Henry said, "Of all graces faith honours Christ most, therefore of all graces Christ honours faith most."[4]

John says that if you have been born of God, then you will believe in His Son. You will love Him and His people, and you will overcome the world. No one but Christ can give you that power. You cannot give it to yourself. The church cannot give it to you. It is a divine gift, which enables you to say, "Whom have I in heaven but thee? and there is none upon earth that I desire beside thee" (Ps. 73:25).

2. *Purifying the heart through Christ-centeredness.* First John 3:3 says that every person who has the Christian hope within himself of being a son of God "purifieth himself, even as he is pure." Faith is a heavenly plant that will not flourish in impure soil. Faith is transforming. A homely person who looks at a beautiful object will remain homely, but a believer who fixes his faith on Christ is transformed into the image of Christ. Faith that looks at a bleeding Christ produces a bleeding heart; faith that looks at a holy Christ produces a holy life; faith that looks at an afflicted Christ produces sanctified affliction. And, according to Richard Cecil, "One affliction sanctified, will do more in enabling the Christian to get a victory over the world, than twenty years of prosperity and peace."

Faith that looks to Christ partakes of His moral excellence. When we look at Christ, the lusts of the world no longer have dominion over us. Worldliness is driven from the heart, its supreme fortress.

Christ overcame sin, Satan, death, and hell *for* us, but he also promises to be *in* us to purify us. That is the secret of overcoming the world, for, as 1 John 4:4 says, "Greater is he that is in you, than he that is in the world."

29

Faith helps us to see sin as it really is. Satan tries to make sin attractive. Sadly, we are prone to yield to that trick. We ask, "What is the harm of listening to 'Christian' contemporary music? Everyone else is doing it." We then take sin as a sweet morsel on our tongue. That will not happen if we put faith to work, for faith sees sin for what it is. "Faith looks behind the curtain of sense, and sees sin before it is dressed up for the stage," wrote William Gurnall.[5] Faith sees the ugliness of sin without its camouflage.

Of course, there will be times when the world appears to be overcoming us. There will be times when we forget that we have conquered our worldly flesh through Christ, times when we fail to live in the freedom granted us through faith. Think of the American Civil War, when the edict of emancipation freed all slaves. Long after the war had been fought and won over that issue, some freedmen went on living like slaves. They simply could not grasp the victory that was theirs. Others loved their masters and chose to willingly serve them as bondslaves.

So it is with us Christians. We have been freed from the slavery of the world through Christ, yet we can live like free people only if we resist the attractions of the world. And the only way we can do it is if we tell the world, by faith, "All that you offer me is passing vanity. I belong to the King of kings, to the One who has triumphed. He gives me solid joys and lasting pleasure. He has bound me to His presence and service as a willing bondslave." When we fail to live according to that sense of victory, we need to be reminded of the Savior's words, "In the world ye shall have tribulation: but be of good cheer; I have overcome the world" (John 16:33).

3. Living according to what pleases God. By faith, we are pleased by what pleases God. We delight in God's delights. And, as our faith grows stronger, it increasingly tramples the world under its feet. It does this by obeying God's commandments. As John says,

30

"This is the love of God, that we keep his commandments . . . *for* whatsoever is born of God overcometh the world" (1 John 5:3–4).

The aim of the world's commandments is to gain wealth, fame, social standing, secular power, and human pleasure. Jesus Christ aimed for none of that. He overcame the world by obeying God's commandments—loving God above all and His neighbor as Himself. That is the goal of all those born of God. They yearn to obey God's commandments. And if we keep God's commandments, we will overcome the world.

We need to avoid two extremes in obeying God's commandments, however. One is legalism, which adds man-made requirements to God's commandments. The other is antinomianism, which denies the authority of the law as a rule of life for Christians. Today, our greatest problem is antinomianism. We will not be ruled by God. We fancy that our own instincts are so sanctified that we can safely follow where they lead. This thinking can lead us into the swift current of worldliness. As soon as a believer rests his oars in his battle to keep God's commandments, he yields to the world and is swept downstream. He is then overcome by the world rather than overcoming the world in Christ.

Faith like that of David and Daniel finds obedience to God's commandments more important than life itself. That's why the apostles, prophets, and martyrs endured all kinds of hardships. They were stoned, sawed asunder, and slain by the sword, but none of those things took away their faith. Rather, they rejoiced that they were counted worthy to suffer for Christ.

When pleasing God becomes more important than pleasing people, the believer overcomes his love for this world's honor, riches, pleasures, entertainments, and friendships. Faith prepares him for submission in losses, self-denial, and enduring afflictions for Christ's sake.

31

4. *Living for the unseen world that awaits us.* Faith refuses to call good evil and evil good. Faith dissolves the world's charms; it sees the world in its true colors, so that the world's control is broken.

Faith also sees the ultimate curse that awaits worldliness. God curses worldliness. John tells us that "the world passeth away, and the lust thereof" (1 John 2:17). The world's best pleasures are temporary. The world is our passage, not our portion. As Hebrews 9:27 says, "It is appointed unto men once to die, but after this the judgment."

This world will one day be burned up, together with all of those who lust after it. What will be left when all the lusts for which people sell their souls, ruin their families, and stain their reputations have passed away? Nothing but dust, ashes, and the wrath of God. As Spurgeon said, "If you had got all the world, you would have got nothing after your coffin lid was screwed down but grave dust in your mouth."

Faith sees that the world is unworthy of our attention. It sees that the world never gives what it promises. It is a gigantic mirage, a tragic fraud, a hollow bubble. "To forsake Christ for the world is to leave a treasure for a trifle, eternity for a moment, reality for a shadow," wrote William Jenkyn.[6]

As John Trapp wrote, "Pleasure, profit, and preferment are the worldling's trinity."[7] Long ago, Solomon discovered all three to be vanity. When you read Ecclesiastes, you will understand why John Bunyan called the world Vanity Fair. You also will realize why James asked: "Know ye not that the friendship of the world is enmity with God? Whosoever therefore will be a friend of the world is the enemy of God" (4:4). William Gurnall summed it well, "The bee will not sit on a flower where no honey can be sucked, neither should the Christian."[8]

Faith sees there are greater pleasures to be had by abstaining from sin than by indulging in it. Faith values the eternal rewards that Christ has laid up in heaven far more than all the treasures of the world (Heb. 11:25–26). In abstaining from worldly pursuits, the Christian experiences true happiness, believing that in God's presence there are "fulness of joy" and "pleasures for evermore" (Ps. 16:11).

3

MAKING THE
OVERCOMING LAST

f we overcome the world, we will be fully delivered from the world in the age to come. Here on earth, heaven is in our hearts and in our deepest affections, yet the world and the devil are at our elbow. But only righteousness will dwell in the new heavens and earth to come. By faith we believe that Christ has gone to prepare that world for us and will return to put an end to the present evil one. Satan and all of his followers will one day be banished to eternal perdition. And the people of God will shine in the firmament of God's glory.

By faith we believe that the best is yet to come. We look to a time when we will be saved forever from Satan, the world, and our old nature. Sin will be left behind; evil will be walled out. There will be no more tears, pain, sorrow, temptation, or death. We will worship and praise God, serve and reign with Christ, and fellowship with the saints and angels. We will find heaven a perfect place of perfect mansions, perfect gold, perfect light, and perfect pleasure. Above all, we will be in perfect communion with the Triune God, knowing, seeing, loving, and praising Him forever. Truly, "our light affliction, which is but for a moment, worketh for us a far more exceeding and eternal weight of glory" (2 Cor. 4:17).

Overcoming the world by faith will last forever. That is because the object of faith is the Son of God, and the author of faith is the Spirit of Christ. The source of strength for the believer does not lie in himself or even in his faith but in the object of that faith, Jesus, the Son of God.

Christ died to cut the cord between sinners and the world. As Galatians 1:4 says, Christ "gave himself for our sins, that he might deliver us from this present evil world, according to the will of God and our Father." Christ didn't come just to deliver His people from eternal condemnation, great as that is, but He came to deliver them from this present evil world. He endured beatings, shame, pain, and rejection to wrench those He calls His own out of this present evil world and into the kingdom of God.

In Galatians 6:14 Paul says, "God forbid that I should glory, save in the cross of our Lord Jesus Christ, by whom the world is crucified unto me, and I unto the world." He is saying that the cross of Jesus Christ is so powerful that it makes the world totally undesirable to him. The world has lost its color for Paul and become completely unappealing because of Christ and future glory.

All of this has much to say to us as believers in a world that seeks to trap us in its pleasures. There are four lessons we should learn if we would persevere in overcoming the world: (1) rely on Jesus to intercede; (2) use every means available; (3) turn to the Lord; and (4) remember God's promise of victory.

Trust Our Great High Priest

When the power of the world threatens to invade our souls, we can take comfort by remembering that our great High Priest prayed, "I pray not that thou shouldest take them out of the world, but that thou shouldest keep them from the evil" (John 17:15). When our defenses are down and we are most vulnerable to yielding to the enemy of our souls, we may hope for deliverance through the intercession of Jesus Christ and His Spirit. We may cry out, "Dear Savior, were it not for Thy intercession, and blessed Spirit, and Thy preservation in the hour of temptation we would have been swept into evil."

Use Every Means to Strengthen Ourselves

We must listen to sermons, saturate ourselves with Scripture, read books that can make us "wise unto salvation," and pray without ceasing. We must fellowship with believers, observe the Lord's Day, evangelize unbelievers, and serve others. We must be good stewards of our time, always remembering, as Thomas Manton said, "A carnal Christian is no Christian but the carcase of a Christian, [for] if we don't put the love of the world to death, the world will put us to death."

When Philip Henry, father of Matthew Henry, was thirty years old, he wrote in his diary, "So old and older than Alexander when he conquered the great world; but I have not subdued the little world of *myself*."[1] Is this your complaint? Do you also repent of your failures?

When we surrender to the devil's temptation, that failure is rooted in unbelief. Usually, we are guilty of neglecting to use the shield of faith and the means of grace to protect us from the enemy. Jesus often asked His disciples, "Where is your faith?" He also asks us whenever we allow the fiery darts of

Satan to enter our soul: "Why don't you believe, watch, and pray?"

A faith that doesn't diligently use God's means of combat is no faith at all, for it does not change us from within. When God and others cannot see a difference in our lives as we move from unbelief to faith, our faith is not real.

Let us beware of anything that is rooted in worldly success, worldly theories, and worldly methods. For example, Christians who trust Christ and His Word should resist turning for help to therapists who approach problems from the world's point of view. Too often psychologists advocate self-reliance rather than reliance on God.

If J. C. Ryle could write in the late nineteenth century, "Worldliness is the peculiar plague of Christendom in our own era," how much more ought we to see it in our day! Myriads of so-called Christians today think like the world, look like the world, and act like the world. They may appear morally decent, but Christ is not the focus of their lives. They are at home in this world and lack a passionate commitment to Christ and His Great Commission. They forget that when the worldly man thinks he has conquered the world, the world has conquered him. Then he is no longer salt and light in the world, and provides evidence that he is not born again after all.

Turn to the Lord

Let's heed Thomas Guthrie, "If you find yourself loving any pleasure better than praying, any book better than the Bible, any house better than the house of God, any table better than the Lord's table, any person better than Christ, any indulgence better than the hope of heaven—take alarm!"[2] Friend, if you marry the spirit of this age, you'll find yourself a widow or widower in the age to come. Don't dress for the world to come in front of the mirror of this world. Remember, repent, return, and do the first works (Rev. 2:4–5).

If you have not been born of God, cry to Him immediately for a new heart. Without being born again, you will never overcome the world but will go to hell with the rest of the world. Turn from your sins and call upon Christ to save you—to give you faith and repentance, and to dwell within you by His Spirit. Pray for faith in Christ and His atoning death so that the world will lie dead at your feet. "Be not conformed to this world: but be ye transformed by the renewing of your mind, that ye may prove what is that good, and acceptable, and perfect, will of God" (Rom. 12:2).

Be Mindful of God's Promise of Victory

Like Christians of every generation, we grapple with besetting sins. Yet God has promised us the victory! Consider the heroes of faith in Hebrews 11. They believed in God amid the worst battles of this world. They put on the "whole armour of God," especially "the shield of faith" and "the sword of the Spirit" (Eph. 6:10–18). So should we. "Be faithful unto death, and I will give you a crown of life," Jesus said.

Consider also Martin Luther, John Calvin, William Carey, David Brainerd, and hosts of less famous believers. On the Great Day of Judgment, hosts of believers will, by God's grace, confess at the throne of the Lamb, "I have fought a good fight, I have finished my course, I have kept the faith: Henceforth there is laid up for me a crown of righteousness, which the Lord, the righteous judge, shall give me at that day: and not to me only, but unto all them also that love his appearing" (2 Tim. 4:7–8). Such are the words and deeds of one who has overcome the world by faith. Amen.

PART 2

OVERCOMING
THE
WORLD
THROUGH
PIETY

Calvin's Answer for Worldliness

WHAT IS PIETY?

*J*ohn Calvin's *Institutes* have earned him the title of "the preeminent systematician of the Protestant Reformation." His reputation as an intellectual, however, is often seen separately from the vital spiritual and pastoral context in which he wrote his theology. For Calvin, theological understanding and practical piety, truth and usefulness, are inseparable. Theology deals first of all with knowledge—knowledge of God and of ourselves; but there is no true knowledge where there is no true piety.

Calvin's concept of piety (*pietas*) is rooted in the knowledge of God and includes attitudes and actions that are directed to the adoration and service of God. In addition, his *pietas* includes a host of related themes, such as love in human relationships and respect for the image of God in human beings. Calvin's piety is evident in people who recognize through experiential faith that they have been accepted in Christ and engrafted into His body by the grace of God. In this "mystical union," the Lord claims them as His own in life and in death. They become God's people and members of Christ by the power of the Holy Spirit. This relationship restores their joy of fellowship with God; it re-creates their lives. It delivers them from the bondage of carnal worldliness.

The purpose of chapters 4–7 is to show that Calvin's piety is a sufficient answer for the problem of worldliness, for his concept of piety conquers the heart. Calvin's piety is biblical, with an emphasis on the heart more than the mind. Head and heart must work together, but the heart is more important.[1] After an introductory look at the definition and goal of piety in Calvin's thinking (ch. 4), we will examine how his *pietas* affects the theological (ch. 5), ecclesiological (ch. 6), and practical (ch. 7) dimensions of his thought.

The Definition and Importance of Piety

Pietas is one of the major themes of Calvin's theology. His theology is, as John T. McNeill says, "his piety described at length."[2] He was determined to confine theology within the limits of piety.[3] In his preface addressed to King Francis I, Calvin says that the purpose of writing the *Institutes* was "solely to transmit certain rudiments by which those who are touched with any zeal for religion might be shaped to true godliness [*pietas*]."[4]

For Calvin, *pietas* designates the right attitude of man toward God. It is an attitude that includes true knowledge, heartfelt worship, saving faith, filial fear, prayerful submission, and reverential love.[5] Knowing who and what God is (theology) embraces right attitudes toward Him and doing what He wants (piety). In his first catechism, Calvin writes, "True piety consists in a sincere feeling which loves God as Father as much as it fears and reverences Him as Lord, embraces His righteousness, and dreads offending Him worse than death."[6] In the *Institutes* Calvin is more succinct, "I call 'piety' that reverence joined with love of God which the knowledge of his benefits induces."[7] This love and reverence for God is a necessary concomitant to any knowledge of Him and embraces all of life. As Calvin says, "The whole life of Christians ought to be a sort of practice of godliness."[8] The subtitle of the first edition of the *Institutes* reads, "Embracing almost the whole sum of piety & whatever is necessary to know of the doctrine of salvation: A work most worthy to be read by all persons zealous for piety."[9]

Calvin's commentaries also reflect the importance of *pietas*. For example, he writes on 1 Timothy 4:7–8: "You will do the thing of greatest value, if with all your zeal and ability you devote yourself to godliness [*pietas*] alone. Godliness is the beginning, middle and end of Christian living. Where it is complete, there is nothing lacking. . . . Thus the conclusion is that we should concentrate exclusively on godliness, for when once we have attained to it, God requires no more of us."[10] Commenting on 2 Peter 1:3, he says, "As soon as he [Peter] has made mention of life he immediately adds godliness [*pietas*] as if it were the soul of life."[11]

Piety's Supreme Goal: Soli Deo Gloria

The goal of piety, as well as the entire Christian life, is the glory of God—glory that shines in God's attributes, in the structure of the world, and in the death and resurrection of Jesus Christ.[12] Glorifying God supersedes personal salvation for every truly pious person.[13] So Calvin writes to Cardinal Sadolet: "It is not very sound theology to confine a man's thought so much to himself, and not to set before him, as the prime motive for his existence, zeal to illustrate the glory of God. . . . I am persuaded that there is no man imbued with true piety who will not consider as insipid that long and labored exhortation to zeal for heavenly life, a zeal which keeps a man entirely devoted to himself and does not, even by one expression, arouse him to sanctify the name of God."[14]

The goal of piety—that God may be glorified in us—is that for which we were created. Thus, the regenerate yearn to live out the purpose of their original creation.[15] The pious man, according to Calvin, confesses, "We are God's: let us therefore live for him and die for him. We are God's: let his wisdom and will therefore rule all our actions. We are God's: let all the parts of our life accordingly strive toward him as our only lawful goal."[16]

God redeems, adopts, and sanctifies His people that His glory might shine in them and deliver them from impious self-seeking.[17] The pious man's deepest concern, therefore, is God Himself and the things of God—God's Word, God's authority, God's gospel, God's truth. He yearns to know more of God and to commune more with Him.

But how do we glorify God? As Calvin writes, "God has prescribed for us a way in which he will be glorified by us, namely, piety, which consists in the obedience of his Word. He that exceeds these bounds does not go about to honor God, but rather to dishonor him."[18] Obedience to God's Word means taking refuge in Christ for forgiveness of our sins, knowing Him through His Word, serving Him with a loving heart, doing good works in gratitude for His goodness, and exercising self-denial to the point of loving our enemies.[19] This response involves total surrender to God Himself, His Word, and His will.[20]

Calvin says, "I offer thee my heart, Lord, promptly and sincerely." That is the desire of all who are truly pious. However, that desire can be realized only through communion with Christ and participation in Him, for outside of Christ even the most religious person lives for himself. Only in Christ can the pious live as willing servants of their Lord, faithful soldiers of their Commander, and obedient children of their Father.[21]

5

COMMUNION WITH CHRIST

alvin's doctrine of union with Christ is one of the most consistently influential features of his theology and ethics, if not the single most important teaching that animates the whole of his thought and his personal life," writes David Willis-Watkins.[1]

Piety's Profound Root: Mystical Union

Calvin did not intend to present theology from the viewpoint of a single doctrine. Nonetheless, his sermons, commentaries, and theological works are so permeated with the doctrine of union with Christ that it becomes the focus for Christian faith and practice.[2] Calvin says as much when he writes, "That joining together of Head and members, that indwelling of Christ in our hearts—in short, that mystical union—are accorded by us the highest degree of importance, so that Christ, having been made ours, makes us sharers with him in the gifts with which he has been endowed."[3]

For Calvin, piety is rooted in the believer's mystical union (*unio mystica*) with Christ; thus this union must be our starting point.[4] That union is possible because Christ took on our human nature, filling it with His virtue. Union with Christ in His humanity is historical, ethical, and personal, but not essential. There is no crass mixture of human substances between Christ and us. Nonetheless, Calvin states, "Not only does he cleave to us by an indivisible bond of fellowship, but with a wonderful communion, day by day, he grows more and more into one body with us, until he becomes completely one with us."[5] This union is one of the gospel's greatest mysteries.[6] Because of the fountain of Christ's perfection in our nature, the pious may, by faith, draw whatever they need for their sanctification. The flesh of Christ is the source from which His people derive life and power.[7]

If Christ had died and risen but did not apply His salvation to believers for their regeneration and sanctification, His work would have been ineffectual. Piety shows that the Spirit of Christ is working in us what has already been accomplished in Christ. Christ administers His sanctification to the church through His royal priesthood so that the church may live piously for Him.[8]

The heartbeat of Calvin's practical theology and piety is communion (*communio*) with Christ. This involves participation (*participatio*) in His benefits, which are inseparable from union with Christ.[9] That emphasis was already evident in the *Confessio Fidei de Eucharistia* (1537), signed by Calvin, Martin Bucer, and Wolfgang Capito.[10] However, Calvin's communion with Christ is not shaped by his doctrine of the Lord's

Supper; rather, his emphasis on spiritual communion with Christ helped shape his concept of the sacrament.

Similarly, the concepts of *communio* and *participatio* helped shape Calvin's understanding of regeneration, faith, justification, sanctification, assurance, election, and the church, for he could not speak of any doctrine apart from communion with Christ. That is the heart of Calvin's system of theology.

Piety's Double Bond with Christ: The Spirit and Faith

Communion with Christ is realized only through Spirit-worked faith. It is actual communion, not because believers participate in the essence of Christ's nature, but because the Spirit of Christ unites believers so intimately to Christ that they become flesh of His flesh and bone of His bone. From God's perspective, the Spirit is the bond between Christ and believers, whereas from our perspective, faith is the bond. These perspectives do not clash with each other, since one of the Spirit's principal operations is to work faith in a sinner.[11]

Only the Spirit can unite Christ in heaven with the believer on earth. Just as in the Incarnation the Spirit united heaven and earth, so in regeneration the Spirit raises the elect from earth to commune with Christ in heaven and brings Christ into the hearts and lives of the elect on earth.[12] Communion with Christ is always the result of the Spirit's work—a work that is astonishing and experiential rather than comprehensible.[13] The Holy Spirit is thus the link that binds the believer to Christ and the channel through which Christ is communicated to the believer.[14] As Calvin writes to Peter Martyr: "We grow up together with Christ into one body, and he shares his Spirit with us, through whose hidden operation he has become ours. Believers receive this communion with Christ at the same time as their calling. But they grow from day to day more and more

47

in this communion, in proportion to the life of Christ growing within them."[15]

Calvin moves beyond Luther in this emphasis on communion with Christ. Calvin stresses that, by His Spirit, Christ empowers those who are united with Him by faith. Being "engrafted into the death of Christ, we derive from it a secret energy, as the twig does from the root," Calvin writes. The believer "is animated by the secret power of Christ; so that Christ may be said to live and grow in him; for as the soul enlivens the body, so Christ imparts life to his members."[16]

Like Luther, Calvin believes that knowledge is fundamental to faith. Such knowledge includes the Word of God as well as the proclamation of the gospel.[17] Since the written Word is exemplified in the living Word, Jesus Christ, in whom all God's promises are fulfilled, faith cannot be separated from Christ.[18] The work of the Spirit does not supplement or supersede the revelation of Scripture, but authenticates it. "Take away the Word, and no faith will remain," Calvin says.[19]

Faith unites the believer to Christ by means of the Word, enabling the believer to receive Christ as He is clothed in the gospel and graciously offered by the Father.[20] By faith, God also dwells in the believer. Consequently, Calvin says, "We ought not to separate Christ from ourselves or ourselves from him," but participate in Christ by faith, for this "revives us from death to make us a new creature."[21]

By faith the believer possesses Christ and grows in Him. What's more, the degree of his faith exercised through the Word determines his degree of communion with Christ.[22] "Everything which faith should contemplate is exhibited to us in Christ," Calvin writes.[23] Though Christ remains in heaven, the believer who excels in piety learns to grasp Christ so firmly by faith that Christ dwells within his heart.[24] By faith the pious live by what they find in Christ rather than by what they find in themselves.[25]

For Calvin, communion with Christ flows out of union with Christ. Looking to Christ for assurance, therefore, means looking at ourselves in Christ. As David Willis-Watkins writes, "Assurance of salvation is a derivative self-knowledge, whose focus remains on Christ as united to his body, the Church, of which we are members."[26]

Piety's Double Cleansing: Justification and Sanctification

According to Calvin, believers receive from Christ by faith the "double grace" of justification and sanctification, which together provide a twofold cleansing.[27] Justification offers imputed purity, and sanctification, actual purity.[28]

Calvin defines justification as "the acceptance with which God receives us into his favor as righteous men."[29] He goes on to say that "since God justifies us by the intercession of Christ, he absolves us not by the confirmation of our own innocence but by the imputation of righteousness, so that we who are not righteous in ourselves may be reckoned as such in Christ."[30] Justification includes the remission of sins and the right to eternal life.

Calvin regards justification as a central doctrine of the Christian faith. He calls it "the principal hinge by which religion is supported," the soil out of which the Christian life develops, and the substance of piety.[31] Justification not only serves God's honor by satisfying the conditions for salvation; it also offers the believer's conscience "peaceful rest and serene tranquility."[32] As Romans 5:1 says, "Therefore being justified by faith, we have peace with God through our Lord Jesus Christ." This is the heart and soul of piety. Because they are justified by faith, believers need not worry about their status with God. They can willingly renounce personal glory and daily accept their life from the hand of their Creator and Redeemer. Daily skirmishes may be lost to the enemy, but Jesus Christ has won the war for them.

Sanctification refers to the process in which the believer increasingly becomes conformed to Christ in heart, conduct, and devotion to God. It is the continual remaking of the believer by the Holy Spirit, the increasing consecration of body and soul to God.[33] In sanctification the believer offers himself to God as a sacrifice. This does not come without great struggle and slow progress. It requires cleansing from the pollution of the flesh and renouncing the world.[34] It requires repentance, mortification, and daily conversion.

Justification and sanctification are inseparable, Calvin says. To separate one from the other is to tear Christ in pieces,[35] or like trying to separate the sun's light from the heat that the light generates.[36] Believers are justified in order to worship God in holiness of life.[37]

PIETY AND THE CHURCH

alvin's *pietas* doesn't stand apart from Scripture or from the church. Rather, it is rooted in the Word and nurtured in the church. While breaking with the clericalism and absolutism of Rome, Calvin nonetheless maintains a high view of the church. "If we do not prefer the church to all other objects of our interest, we are unworthy of being counted among her members," he writes.

Augustine once said, "He cannot have God for his Father who refuses to have the church for his mother." To that Calvin adds, "For there is no other way to enter into life unless this mother conceive us in her womb, give us birth, nourish us at her breast, and lastly, unless she keep us under her care and guidance until, putting off mortal flesh, we become like the angels." Apart from the church, there is little hope for forgiveness of sins or salvation, Calvin wrote. It is always disastrous to leave the church.[1]

Calvin taught that believers are engrafted into Christ and His church, for spiritual growth happens within the church. The church is mother, educator, and nourisher of every believer, for the Holy Spirit acts in her. Believers cultivate piety by the Spirit through the church's teaching ministry, progressing from spiritual infancy to adolescence to full adulthood in Christ. They do not graduate from the church until they die.[2] This life-long education is offered within an atmosphere of genuine piety in which believers love and care for one another under the headship of Christ.[3] It encourages the growth of one another's gifts and love, as we are "constrained to borrow from others."[4]

Growth in piety is impossible apart from the church, for piety is fostered by the communion of saints. Within the church, believers "cleave to each other in the mutual distribution of gifts."[5] Each member has his own place and gifts to use within the body.[6] Ideally, the entire body uses these gifts in symmetry and proportion, ever reforming and growing toward perfection.[7]

Piety of the Word

The Word of God is central to the development of Christian piety in the believer. Genuine piety is a "piety of the Word." Calvin's relational model explains how.

True religion is a dialogue between God and man. The part of the dialogue that God initiates is revelation. In this, God comes down to meet us, addresses us, and makes Himself known to us in the preaching of the Word. The other part of the dialogue is man's response to God's revelation. This response, which includes trust, adoration, and godly fear, is what Calvin calls *pietas*. The preaching of the Word saves us and preserves us as the Spirit enables us to appropriate the blood of Christ and respond to Him with reverential love. By the Spirit-empowered preaching of men "the renewal of the saints is accomplished and the body of Christ is edified," Calvin says.[8] The preaching of the Word is our spiritual food and our medicine for spiritual health. With the Spirit's blessing, ministers are spiritual physicians who apply the Word to our souls as earthly physicians apply medicine to our bodies. With the Word these spiritual doctors diagnose, prescribe for, and cure spiritual disease in those plagued by sin and death. The preached Word is used as an instrument to heal, cleanse, and make fruitful our disease-prone souls.[9] The Spirit, or the "internal minister," promotes piety by using the "external minister" to preach the Word. As Calvin says, the external minister "holds forth the vocal word and it is received by the ears," but the internal minister "truly communicates the thing proclaimed . . . that is Christ."[10]

To promote piety, the Spirit not only uses the gospel to work faith deep within the souls of His elect, as we have already seen, but He also uses the law. The law promotes piety in three ways:

1. It restrains sin and promotes righteousness in the church and society, preventing both from lapsing into chaos.

2. It disciplines, educates, convicts, and drives us outside of ourselves to Jesus Christ, the fulfiller and end of the law. The law cannot lead us to a saving knowledge of God in Christ. Rather, the Holy Spirit uses the law as a mirror to show us our guilt, to shut us off from hope, and to bring us to repentance. It drives us to the spiritual need out of which faith in Christ is born. This convicting use of the law is critical for the believer's piety, for it prevents the ungodly self-righteousness that is prone to reassert itself even in the holiest of saints.

OVERCOMING THE WORLD THROUGH PIETY

3. It becomes the rule of life for the believer. "What is the rule of life which [God] has given us?" Calvin asks in the Genevan Catechism. The answer: "His law." Later, Calvin says the law "shows the mark at which we ought to aim, the goal towards which we ought to press, that each of us, according to the measure of grace bestowed upon him, may endeavor to frame his life according to the highest rectitude, and, by constant study, continually advance more and more.[11]

   Calvin writes about the third use of the law in the first edition of his *Institutes*: "Believers . . . profit by the law because from it they learn more thoroughly each day what the Lord's will is like. . . . It is as if some servant, already prepared with complete earnestness of heart to commend himself to his master, must search out and oversee his master's ways in order to conform and accommodate himself to them. Moreover, however much they may be prompted by the Spirit and eager to obey God, they are still weak in the flesh, and would rather serve sin than God. The law is to this flesh like a whip to an idle and balky ass, to goad, stir, arouse it to work."[12]

   In the last edition of the *Institutes* (1559), Calvin is more emphatic about how believers profit from the law. First, he says, "Here is the best instrument for them to learn more thoroughly each day the nature of the Lord's will to which they aspire, and to confirm them in the understanding of it." And second, it causes the servant of God "by frequent meditation upon it to be aroused to obedience, be strengthened in it, and be drawn back from the slippery path of transgression." In this way the saints must press on, Calvin concludes. "For what would be less lovable than the law if, with importuning and threatening alone, it troubled souls through fear, and distressed them through fright?"[13]

The view of the law primarily as a guide that encourages the believer to cling to God and obey Him illustrates another instance where Calvin differs from Luther. For Luther, the law is primarily negative. It is closely linked with sin, death, and the devil. Luther's dominant interest is in the second, convicting use of the law—even when he considers the law's role in sanctification. By contrast, Calvin views the law primarily as a positive expression of the will of God. As John Hesselink says, "Calvin's view could be called Deuteronomic, for to him law and love are not antithetical, but are correlates."[14] For Calvin, the believer follows God's law, not out of compulsory obedience, but out of grateful obedience. Under the tutelage of the Spirit, the law prompts gratitude in the believer, which leads to loving obedience and aversion to sin. In other words, for Luther the primary purpose of the law is to help the believer recognize and confront sin. For Calvin the primary purpose of the law is to direct the believer to serve God out of love.[15]

Piety in the Sacraments

Calvin defines the sacraments as testimonies "of divine grace toward us, confirmed by an outward sign, with mutual attestation of our piety toward him."[16] The sacraments are "exercises of piety." The sacraments strengthen our faith and help us offer ourselves as a living sacrifice to God.

For Calvin, as for Augustine, the sacraments are the visible Word. The preached Word comes through our ears; the visible Word, through our eyes. The sacraments hold forth the same Christ as the preached Word but communicate Him through a different mode.

In the sacraments God accommodates Himself to our weakness. When we hear the Word indiscriminately proclaimed, we may wonder: "Is it truly for me? Does it really

OVERCOMING THE WORLD THROUGH PIETY

reach me?" However, in the sacraments God reaches out and touches us individually, and says, "Yes, it's for *you*. The promise extends to *you*." The sacraments thus minister to our weakness by personalizing the promises for those who trust Christ for salvation.

In the sacraments God comes to His people, encourages them, enables them to know Christ better, builds them up, and nourishes them in Him. Baptism promotes piety as a symbol of how believers are engrafted into Christ, renewed by the Spirit, and adopted into the family of the heavenly Father.[17] Likewise, the Lord's Supper shows how these adopted children are fed by their loving Father. Calvin loves to refer to the Supper as nourishment for the soul. "The signs are bread and wine which represent for us the invisible food that we receive from the flesh and blood of Christ," he says. "Christ is the only food of our soul, and therefore our heavenly Father invites us to Christ, that refreshed by partaking of him, we may repeatedly gather strength until we shall have reached heavenly immortality."[18]

As believers, we need constant nourishment. We never reach a point where we no longer need to hear the Word, to pray, or to be nurtured by the sacraments. We must constantly grow and develop. As we continue to sin because of our old nature, we are in constant need of forgiveness and grace. So the Supper, along with the preaching of the Word, repeatedly says to us: We need Christ, we need to be renewed in Christ and built up in Him. The sacraments promise that Christ is present to receive us, bless us, and renew us.

For Calvin, the word *conversion* doesn't mean just the initial act of coming to faith; it also means daily renewal and growth in following Christ. The sacraments lead the way to this daily conversion. They tell us that we need the grace of Christ every day. We must draw strength from Christ, particularly through the body that He sacrificed for us on the cross.

PIETY AND THE CHURCH

Calvin writes, "For as the eternal Word of God is the fountain of life, so his flesh is the channel to pour out to us the life which resides intrinsically in his divinity. For in his flesh was accomplished man's redemption, in it a sacrifice was offered to atone for sin, and obedience yielded to God to reconcile him to us. It was also filled with the sanctification of the Holy Spirit. Finally having overcome death he was received into the heavenly glory."[19] In other words, the Spirit sanctified Christ's body, which Christ offered on the cross to atone for sin. That body was raised from the dead and received up into heaven. At every stage of our redemption, Christ's body is the pathway to God. In the Supper, then, Christ comes to us and says: "My body is still given for you. By faith you may commune with me and my body and all of its saving benefits."

Calvin teaches that Christ gives Himself to us in the Supper, not just His benefits, just as He gives us Himself and His benefits in the preaching of the Word. Christ also makes us part of His body as He gives us Himself. Calvin cannot precisely explain how that happens in the Supper, for it is better experienced than explained.[20] However, he does say that Christ does not leave heaven to enter the bread. Rather, in the Holy Supper we are called to lift up our hearts on high to heaven, where Christ is, and not cling to the external bread and wine.

We are lifted up through the work of the Holy Spirit in our hearts. As Calvin writes, "Christ, then, is absent from us in respect of his body, but dwelling in us by his Spirit, he raises us to heaven to himself, transfusing into us the vivifying vigor of his flesh just as the rays of the sun invigorate us by its vital warmth."[21] Partaking of the flesh of Christ is a spiritual act rather than a carnal act that involves a "transfusion of substance."[22]

The sacraments can be seen as ladders by which we climb to heaven. "Because we are unable to fly high enough to draw near to God, he has ordained sacraments for us, like ladders,"

Calvin says. "If a man wishes to leap on high, he will break his neck in the attempt, but if he has steps, he will be able to proceed with confidence. So also, if we are to reach our God, we must use the means which he has instituted since he knows what is suitable for us. God has then given us this wonderful support and encouragement and strength in our weakness."[23]

We must never worship the bread because Christ is not *in* the bread; rather, we find Christ *through* the bread. Just as our mouths receive bread to nourish our physical bodies, so our souls, by faith, receive Christ's body and blood to nourish our spiritual lives.

When we commune with Christ through the sacraments, we grow in grace. That's why they are called a means of grace. The sacraments encourage us in our progress toward heaven. They promote confidence in God's promises through Christ's "signified and sealed" redemptive death. Since the sacraments are covenants, they contain promises by which "consciences may be roused to an assurance of salvation," Calvin says.[24] The Spirit enables the believer to "see" the Word engraved upon the sacraments and receive the "peace of conscience" and "a special assurance" offered to him through them.[25]

Finally, the sacraments promote piety by prompting us to thank and praise God for His abundant grace. The sacraments also require us to "attest our piety toward him." As Calvin says, "The Lord recalls the great bounty of his goodness to our memory and stirs us up to acknowledge it; and at the same time he admonishes us not to be ungrateful for such lavish liberality, but rather to proclaim it with fitting praises and to celebrate [the Lord's Supper] by giving thanks."[26]

Two things happen in the Supper: the receiving of Christ and the surrender of the believer. The Lord's Supper is not eucharistic from God's perspective, Calvin says, for Christ is not offered afresh. Nor is it eucharistic in terms of man's merit, for we can offer God nothing by way of sacrifice. But it is eucharistic in terms of our thanksgiving.[27] That sacrifice is an indispensable part of the Lord's Supper which includes "all the duties of love."[28] The Eucharist is an *agapē* feast in which communicants cherish each other and testify of the bond that they enjoy with fellow believers in the unity of the body of Christ.[29]

We offer this sacrifice of gratitude in response to Christ's sacrifice for us. We surrender our lives in response to the heavenly banquet God spreads for us in the Supper. By the Spirit's grace, the Supper enables us as a royal priesthood to offer ourselves as a living sacrifice of praise and thanksgiving to God.[30]

The Lord's Supper thus prompts both piety of grace and piety of gratitude, as Brian Gerrish has shown.[31] The Father's liberality and His children's grateful response are a recurrent theme in Calvin's theology. "We should so revere such a Father with grateful piety and burning love," Calvin admonishes us, "as to devote ourselves wholly to his obedience and honor him in everything."[32] The Supper is the liturgical enactment of grace and gratitude, which lie at the heart of piety.[33]

In the Lord's Supper, these human and divine elements of piety are held in dynamic tension. In that dynamic interchange, God moves toward the believer while His Spirit consummates the Word-based union. At the same time, the believer moves toward God by contemplating the Savior who refreshes and strengthens him. In this, God is glorified and the believer edified.[34]

Piety in the Psalter

Calvin views the Psalms as the canonical manual of piety. In the preface to his five-volume commentary on the Psalms— his largest exposition of any Bible book, Calvin writes: "There is no other book in which we are more perfectly taught the right manner of praising God, or in which we are more powerfully stirred up to the performance of this exercise of piety."[35]

Calvin's preoccupation with the Psalter was motivated by his belief that the Psalms teach and inspire genuine piety in a variety of ways:

- As the revelation from God, the Psalms teach us about God. Because they are theological as well as doxological, they are our sung creed.[36]
- They clearly teach our need for God. They tell us who we are and why we need God's help.[37]
- They offer the divine remedy for our needs. They present Christ in His person, offices, sufferings, death, resurrection, and ascension. They announce the way of salvation, proclaiming the blessedness of justification by faith alone and the necessity of sanctification by the Spirit with the Word.[38]
- They demonstrate God's amazing goodness and invite us to meditate on His grace and mercy. They lead us to repent and fear God, to trust in His Word, and to hope in His mercy.
- They teach us to flee to the God of salvation through prayer, and show us how to bring our requests to God.[39] They show us how to pray confidently in the midst of adversity.[40]
- They show us the depth of communion we may enjoy with our covenant-keeping God. They show how the living church is God's bride, God's children, and God's flock (Ps. 100:3).
- They provide a vehicle for communal worship. Many psalms use first-person plural pronouns ("we," "our") to indicate this communal aspect, but even those with first-person singular pronouns include all those who love the Lord and are committed to Him. They move us to trust and praise God and to love our neighbors.

- They prompt reliance on God's promises, zeal for God and His house, and compassion for the suffering.
- They cover the full range of spiritual experience, including faith and unbelief, joy in God and sorrow over sin, divine presence and divine desertion. As Calvin says, they are "an anatomy of all parts of the soul."[41] We see our own affections and spiritual maladies in the words of the psalmists. When we read about their experiences, we are drawn to self-examination and faith by the grace of the Spirit. The psalms of David, especially, are like a mirror in which we are led to praise God and find rest in His sovereign purposes.[42]

Calvin immersed himself in the Psalms for twenty-five years as a commentator, preacher, biblical scholar, and worship leader.[43] Early on, he began work on metrical versions of the Psalms to be used in public worship. On January 16, 1537, shortly after his arrival in Geneva, Calvin asked his council to introduce the singing of psalms into church worship. He recruited the talents of other men, such as Clement Marot, Louis Bourgeois, and Theodore Beza, to produce the Genevan Psalter. That work took twenty-five years to complete. The first collection (1539) contained eighteen psalms, six of which Calvin put into verse. The rest were done by the French poet Marot. An expanded version containing thirty-five psalms was next (1542), followed by one of forty-nine psalms (1543). Calvin wrote the preface to both of those, commending the practice of congregational singing. After Marot's death in 1544, Calvin encouraged Beza to put the rest of the psalms into verse. In 1562, two years before his death, Calvin rejoiced to see the first complete edition of the Genevan Psalter.[44]

The Genevan Psalter is furnished with a remarkable collection of 125 melodies, written specifically for the Psalms by outstanding musicians, of whom Louis Bourgeois is the best

61

known. The tunes are melodic, distinctive, and reverent.[45] They clearly express Calvin's convictions that piety is best promoted when priority is given to text over tune, while recognizing that the Psalms deserve their own music. Since music should help the reception of the Word, Calvin says, it should be "weighty, dignified, majestic, and modest"—fitting attitudes for a sinful creature in the presence of God.[46] This protects the sovereignty of God in worship and offers proper conformity between the believer's inward disposition and his outward confession.

Psalm-singing is one of the four principal acts of church worship, Calvin believed. It is an extension of prayer. It is also the most significant vocal contribution of people in the service. Psalms were sung in Sunday morning and Sunday afternoon services. Beginning in 1546, a printed table indicated which psalms were to be sung on each occasion. They were assigned to each service according to the texts that were preached. By 1562, three psalms were sung at each service.[47]

Calvin believed that corporate singing subdued the fallen heart and retrained wayward affections in the way of piety. Like preaching and the sacraments, psalm-singing disciplines the heart's affections in the school of faith and lifts the believer to God. Psalm-singing amplifies the effect of the Word upon the heart and multiplies the spiritual energy of the church. "The Psalms can stimulate us to raise our hearts to God and arouse us to an ardor in invoking as well as in exalting with praises the glory of his name," Calvin wrote.[48] With the Spirit's direction, psalm-singing tunes the hearts of believers for glory.

The Genevan Psalter was an integral part of Calvinist worship for centuries. It set the standard for succeeding French Reformed psalm books as well as those in English, Dutch, German, and Hungarian. As a devotional book, it warmed the hearts of thousands though the people who sang from it understood that its power wasn't in the book itself or its words, but in the Spirit who impressed those words on their hearts.

The Genevan Psalter promoted piety by stimulating a spirituality of the Word that was corporate and liturgical, and that broke down the distinction between liturgy and life. The Calvinists freely sang the psalms not only in their churches, but also in homes and workplaces, on the streets, and in the fields.[49] The singing of psalms became a "means of Huguenot self-identification."[50] This pious exercise became a cultural emblem. In short, as T. Hartley Hall writes, "In scriptural or metrical versions, the Psalms, together with the stately tunes to which they were early set, are clearly the heart and soul of Reformed piety."[51]

PIETY AND THE
BELIEVER

Although Calvin viewed the church as the nursery of piety, he also emphasized the need for personal piety. The Christian strives for piety because he loves righteousness, longs to live to God's glory, and delights to obey God's rule of righteousness set forth in Scripture.[1] God Himself is the focal point of the Christian life[2]—a life that is therefore carried out essentially in self-denial, particularly expressed in Christlike cross-bearing.[3]

For Calvin, such piety "is the beginning, middle, and end of Christian living."[4] It involves numerous practical dimensions for daily Christian living, which are explained thoroughly in Calvin's *Institutes,* commentaries, sermons, letters, and treatises. Here's the gist of what Calvin says on prayer, repentance, and obedience as well as on pious Christian living in chapters 6–10 of book 3 of the *Institutes* of 1559.[5]

Prayer

Prayer is the principal and perpetual exercise of faith and the chief element of piety.[6] Prayer shows God's grace to the believer even as the believer offers praises to God and asks for His faithfulness. It demonstrates and corroborates piety, both privately and corporately.[7]

Calvin devoted the second longest chapter of the *Institutes* (3:20) to prayer. There are six purposes of prayer, according to Calvin: to fly to God with every need, to set all our petitions before God, to prepare us to receive God's benefits with humble gratitude, to meditate upon God's kindness, to instill the proper spirit of delight for God's answers in prayer, and to confirm His providence.[8]

Two problems are likely to surface with Calvin's doctrine of prayer. First, when the believer obediently submits to God's will, he does not necessarily give up his own will. Rather, through the act of submissive prayer, the believer invokes God's providence to act on his behalf. Thus, man's will, under the Spirit's guidance, and God's will work together in communion.

Second, to the objection that prayer seems superfluous in light of God's omniscience and omnipotence, Calvin responds that God ordained prayer more for man as an exercise of piety than for Himself. Providence must be understood in the sense that God ordains the means along with the ends. Prayer is a means to receive what God has planned to bestow.[9] Prayer is a way in which believers seek out and receive what God has determined to do for them from eternity.[10]

Calvin treats prayer as a given rather than a problem. Right prayer is governed by rules. These include praying with:

- a heartfelt sense of reverence
- a sense of need and repentance
- a surrender of all confidence in self and a humble plea for pardon
- a confident hope

All four rules are repeatedly violated by even the holiest of God's people. Nevertheless, for Christ's sake, God does not desert the pious but has mercy for them.[11]

Despite the shortcomings of believers, prayer is required for the increase of piety, for prayer diminishes self-love and multiplies dependence upon God. As the due exercise of piety, prayer unites God and man—not in substance, but in will and purpose. Like the Lord's Supper, prayer lifts the believer to Christ and renders proper glory to God. That glory is the purpose of the first three petitions of the Lord's Prayer as well as other petitions dealing with His creation. Since creation looks to God's glory for its preservation, the entire Lord's Prayer is directed to God's glory.[12]

In the Lord's Prayer, Christ "supplies words to our lips."[13] His prayer shows us how all our prayers must be controlled, formed, and inspired by the Word of God. This alone can provide holy boldness in prayer, "which rightly accords with fear, reverence, and solicitude."[14]

We must be disciplined and steadfast in prayer, for prayer keeps us in fellowship with Christ. We are reassured in prayer of Christ's intercessions without which our prayers would be rejected.[15] Only Christ can turn God's throne of dreadful glory into a throne of grace, to which we can draw near in prayer.[16] Prayer is the channel between God and man. It is the way in which the Christian expresses his praise and adoration of God as well as asks for God's help in submissive piety.[17]

Repentance

Repentance is the fruit of faith and prayer. Luther said in his *Ninety-Five Theses* that all of the Christian life should be marked by repentance. Calvin also sees repentance as a lifelong process. Repentance is not merely the start of the Christian life; it *is* the Christian life. Repentance involves confession of sin as well as growth in holiness. Repentance is the lifelong response of the believer to the gospel in outward life, mind, heart, attitude, and will.[18]

Repentance begins with turning to God from the heart and proceeds from a pure, earnest fear of God. It involves dying to self and sin (mortification) and coming alive to righteousness (vivification) in Christ.[19] Calvin does not limit repentance to an inward grace but views it as the redirection of a man's entire being to righteousness. Without a pure, earnest fear of God, a man will not be aware of the heinousness of sin or want to die to it. Mortification is essential because, though sin ceases to reign in the believer, it does not cease to dwell in him. Romans 7:14–25 shows that mortification is a lifelong process. With the Spirit's help, the believer must put sin to death every day through self-denial, cross-bearing, and meditation on the future life.

Repentance is, however, also characterized by newness of life. Mortification is the means to vivification, which Calvin defines as "the desire to live in a holy and devoted manner, a desire arising from rebirth; as if it were said that man dies to himself that he may begin to live to God."[20] True self-denial results in a life devoted to justice and mercy. The pious both "cease to do evil" and "learn to do well." Through repentance, they bow in the dust before their holy Judge, then are raised up to participate in the life, death, righteousness, and intercession of their Savior. As Calvin writes, "For if we truly partake in his death, 'our old man is crucified by his power, and the body of sin perishes' (Rom. 6:6), that the corruption of original nature may no longer thrive. If we share in his resurrection, through it we are raised up into newness of life to correspond with the righteousness of God."[21]

The words Calvin uses to describe the pious Christian life (*reparatio, regeneratio, reformatio, renovatio, restitutio*) point back to our original state of righteousness. They indicate that a life of *pietas* is restorative in nature. Through Spirit-worked repentance, believers are restored into the image of God.[22]

Self-Denial

Self-denial is the sacrificial dimension of *pietas*. We have seen that piety is rooted in the believer's union with Christ. The fruit of that union is self-denial, which includes the following:

- The realization that we are not our own, but belong to God. We live and die unto Him, according to the rule of His Word. Thus, self-denial is not self-centered, as was often the case in medieval monasticism, but God-centered.[23] Our greatest enemy is neither the devil nor the world but ourselves.

- The desire to seek the things of the Lord throughout our lives. Self-denial leaves no room for pride, lasciviousness, and worldliness. It is the opposite of self-love because it is love for God.[24] The entire orientation of our life must be toward God.

- The commitment to yield ourselves and everything we own to God as a living sacrifice. We then are prepared to love others and to esteem them better than ourselves—not by viewing them as they are in themselves, but by seeing the image of God in them. This uproots our love of strife and self and replaces it with a spirit of gentleness and helpfulness.[25] Our love for others then flows from the heart, and our only limit to helping them is the limit of our resources.[26]

Believers are encouraged to persevere in self-denial by the gospel's promises of the future consummation of the kingdom of God. Such promises help us overcome every obstacle that opposes self-renunciation and assist us in bearing adversity.[27]

Furthermore, self-denial helps us find true happiness because it helps us do what we were created for. We were created to love God above all and our neighbor as ourselves. Restoring that principle results in our happiness. As Calvin says, without self-denial we may possess everything without possessing one particle of real happiness.

Cross-Bearing

While self-denial focuses on inward conformity to Christ, cross-bearing centers on outward Christlikeness. Those who are in fellowship with Christ must prepare themselves for a hard, toilsome life filled with many kinds of evil. The reason for this is not simply sin's effect on this fallen world, but the believer's union with Christ. Because His life was a perpetual cross, ours must also include suffering.[28] We thereby not only participate in the benefits of His atoning work on the cross, but we also experience the Spirit's work of transforming us into the image of Christ.[29]

Cross-bearing tests piety. Through cross-bearing we are roused to hope, trained in patience, instructed in obedience, and chastened for our pride. Cross-bearing is our medicine and our chastisement. We are shown the feebleness of our flesh and taught to suffer for the sake of righteousness.[30]

Happily, God promises to be with us in all our sufferings. He even transforms suffering associated with persecution into comfort and blessing.[31]

Meditation on the Future Life

Through cross-bearing we learn to have contempt for the present life when compared to the blessings of heaven. This life is nothing compared to what is to come. It is like smoke or a shadow. "If heaven is our homeland, what else is the earth but our place of exile? If departure from the world is entry into life, what else is the world but a sepulcher?" Calvin asks.[32] "No one has made progress in the school of Christ who does not joyfully await the day of death and final resurrection."[33]

Typically, Calvin uses the *complexio oppositorum* when explaining the Christian's relation to this world. In other words, he presents opposites to find a middle way between. So, on the one hand, through cross-bearing we are crucified to the world and the world to us. On the other hand, the devout Christian enjoys this present life, albeit with due restraint and moderation, for he is taught to use the things in this world for the purpose that God intended. Calvin was no ascetic; he enjoyed good literature, good food, and the beauties of nature. But he rejected all forms of earthly excess. The believer is called to Christlike moderation, which includes modesty, prudence, avoidance of display, and contentment with our lot.[34] For it is the hope of the life to come that gives purpose to and enjoyment in our present life. This life is always straining after a better, heavenly life.[35]

How, then, is it possible for the truly pious Christian to maintain a proper balance, enjoying the gifts that God gives in this world while avoiding the snare of overindulgence? Calvin offers four guiding principles:

1. Recognize that God is the giver of every good and perfect gift. This should restrain our lusts because our gratitude to God for His gifts cannot be expressed by a greedy reception of them.

2. Understand that if we have few possessions, we must bear our poverty patiently lest we be ensnared by inordinate desire.

3. Remember that we are stewards of the world in which God has placed us. Soon we will have to give an account to Him of our stewardship.

4. Know that God has called us to Himself and to His service. Because of that calling, we strive to fulfill our tasks in His service, for His glory, and under His watchful, benevolent eye.[36]

Obedience

For Calvin, unconditional obedience to God's will is the essence of piety. Piety links love, freedom, and discipline by subjecting all to the will and Word of God.[37] Love is the overarching principle that prevents piety from degenerating into legalism. At the same time, law provides the content for love.

Piety includes rules that govern the believer's response. Privately, those rules can take the form of self-denial and cross-bearing; publicly, they can be expressed in the exercise of church discipline, which Calvin implemented in Geneva. In either case, the glory of God compels disciplined obedience. To Calvin, the pious Christian is neither weak nor passive but dynamically active in the pursuit of obedience, much like a long-distance runner, a diligent scholar, or a heroic warrior submitting to God's will.[38]

In the preface to his commentary on the Psalms, Calvin writes: "Here is the true proof of obedience, where, bidding

71

farewell to our own affections, we subject ourselves to God and allow our lives to be so governed by his will that things most bitter and harsh to us—because they come from him—become sweet to us."[39] "Sweet obedience"—Calvin welcomed such descriptions. According to John Hesselink, Calvin used words such as *sweet, sweetly, sweetness* hundreds of times in his *Institutes,* commentaries, sermons, and treatises to describe the life of piety. Calvin writes of the sweetness of the law, the sweetness of Christ, the sweetness of consolation in the midst of adversity and persecution, the sweetness of prayer, the sweetness of the Lord's Supper, the sweetness of God's free offer of eternal life in Christ, and the sweetness of eternal glory.[40]

He writes of the sweet fruit of election, too, saying that this world and all its glories will ultimately pass away. What gives us assurance of salvation here and hope for the life to come is that we have been "chosen . . . in [Christ] before the foundation of the world" (Eph. 1:4).[41] "We shall never be clearly persuaded . . . that our salvation flows from the wellspring of God's free mercy until we come to know the very sweet fruit of God's eternal election."[42]

Calvin as Exemplar of Piety

Calvin strove to live the life of *pietas* himself—theologically, ecclesiastically, and practically. At the end of his *Life of Calvin,* Theodore Beza wrote, "Having been a spectator of his conduct for sixteen years, . . . I can now declare, that in him all men may see a most beautiful example of the Christian character, an example which it is as easy to slander as it is difficult to imitate."[43]

Calvin shows us the piety of a warmhearted Reformed theologian who speaks from the heart. Having tasted the goodness and grace of God in Jesus Christ, he pursued piety by seeking to know and do God's will every day. He communed with Christ; practiced repentance, self-denial, and cross-bearing; and was involved in vigorous social improvements.[44] His theology worked itself out in heartfelt, Christ-centered piety.[45]

For Calvin and the Reformers of sixteenth-century Europe, doctrine and prayer as well as faith and worship are integrally connected. For Calvin, the Reformation includes the reform of piety (*pietas*), or spirituality, as much as a reform of theology. The spirituality that had been cloistered behind monastery walls for centuries had broken down. Medieval spirituality was reduced to a celibate, ascetic, and penitential devotion in the convent or monastery. But Calvin helped Christians understand that the pious live *coram Deo*, "in the presence of God," from the heart and in daily life. Piety is, therefore, voluntary and unforced, motivated by delight in God. The pious willingly live and act every day according to God's will (Rom. 12:1–2) in the midst of human society. Through Calvin's influence, Protestant spirituality focused on how one lived the Christian life in the family, the fields, the workshop, and the marketplace.[46] Calvin helped the Reformation change the entire focus of the Christian life.

Calvin's teaching, preaching, and catechizing fostered growth in the relationship between believers and God. Piety means experiencing sanctification as a divine work of renewal, expressed in repentance and righteousness, which progresses through conflict and adversity in a Christlike manner. In such piety, prayer and worship are central, both privately and in the community of believers.

The worship of God is always primary, for one's relationship to God takes precedence over everything else. That worship, however, is expressed in how the believer lives his vocation and how he treats his neighbors, for one's relationship with God is most concretely seen in the transformation of every human relationship. Faith and prayer, because they transform every believer, cannot be hidden. Ultimately, therefore, they must transform the church, the community, and the world. Worldliness must surrender to the all-encompassing power of free, unconstrained piety, which yearns to honor God from the heart simply because God is delightful and worthy to be honored. By grace, Calvin's answer for worldliness is successful, for awed love of the Triune God (piety) is more than a match for carnal love of the world (impiety).

PART 3

OVERCOMING

THE

WORLD

THROUGH

HOLINESS

8

THE CALL TO
CULTIVATE HOLINESS

he godly farmer who plows his field, sows seed, fertilizes and cultivates, is acutely aware that in the final analysis, he is utterly dependent on forces outside of himself for an assured crop. He knows he cannot cause the seed to germinate, the rain to fall, or the sun to shine. But he pursues his task with diligence nonetheless, looking to God for blessing, and knowing that if he does not fertilize and cultivate the sown seed, his crop will be meager at best.

Similarly, the Christian life is like a garden that must be cultivated in order to produce the fruits of holy living unto God. "Theology is the doctrine or teaching of living to God," wrote William Ames in the opening words of his classic *The Marrow of Theology*.[1] God Himself exhorts His children, "Be ye holy; for I am holy" (1 Peter 1:16). Paul instructs the Thessalonians,

"God hath not called us unto uncleanness, but unto holiness" (1 Thess. 4:7). And the author of Hebrews writes, "Follow peace with all men, and holiness, without which no man shall see the Lord" (Heb. 12:14). The believer who does not diligently cultivate holiness will neither have much genuine assurance of his own salvation nor be obeying Peter's call to seek it (2 Peter 1:10).[2] In the following chapters we will focus on the Christian's scriptural call to cultivate Spirit-worked holiness by diligently using the means God has provided to assist him.

Holiness is a noun that relates to the adjective *holy* and the verb *sanctify*, which means to "make holy."[3] In biblical languages *holy* means separated and set apart for God. For the Christian, to be set apart means, negatively, to be separate from sin, and, positively, to be consecrated (i.e., dedicated) to God and conformed to Christ. There is no disparity between the Old Testament and New Testament concepts of holiness, though there is a change in emphasis on what holiness involves. The Old Testament stresses ritual and moral holiness; the New Testament stresses inward and transforming holiness (Lev. 10:10–11; 19:2; Heb. 10:10; 1 Thess. 5:23).[4]

Scripture presents the essence of holiness primarily in relation to God. The focus of the sacred realm in Scripture is God Himself. God's holiness is the very essence of His being (Isa. 57:15);[5] it is the backdrop of all else the Bible declares about God. His justice is holy justice; His wisdom is holy wisdom; His power is holy power; His grace is holy grace. No other attribute of God is celebrated before the throne of heaven as is His holiness: "Holy, holy, holy, is the LORD of hosts" (Isa. 6:3). "Holy" is prefixed to God's name more than any other attribute.[6] Isaiah alone calls God the "Holy One" twenty-six times. God's holiness, John Howe wrote, "may be said to be a transcendental attribute that, as it were, runs through the rest, and casts lustre upon them. It is an attribute of attributes . . . and so it is the very lustre and glory of His other perfections."[7] God manifests His majestic holiness in His works (Ps. 145:17), in His law (Ps. 19:8–9), and especially at the cross of Christ (Matt. 27:46). Holiness is His permanent crown, His glory, His beauty. It is "more than a mere attribute of God," says Jonathan Edwards. "It is the sum of all His attributes, the outshining of all that God is."[8]

God's holiness denotes two critical truths about Himself: first, it denotes the "separateness" of God from all His creation and His "apartness" from all that is unclean or evil. God's holiness testifies of His purity, His absolute moral perfection or excellence, His separateness from all outside of Him, and His complete dissociation from sin (Job 34:10; Isa. 5:16; 40:18; Hab. 1:13).[9]

Second, since God is holy and set apart from all sin, He is unapproachable by sinners apart from holy sacrifice (Lev. 17:11; Heb. 9:22). He cannot be the Holy One and remain indifferent to sin (Jer. 44:4); He must punish sin (Ex. 34:6–7). Since all mankind are sinners through both our tragic fall in Adam and our daily transgressions, God can never be appeased by our self-efforts. We creatures, once made after the image of our holy Creator, voluntarily chose in our covenant head Adam to become unholy and unacceptable in the sight of our Creator. Atoning blood must be shed if remission of sin is to be granted (Heb. 9:22). Only the perfect, atoning obedience of a sufficient Mediator, the God-man Christ Jesus, can fulfill the demands of God's holiness on behalf of sinners (1 Tim. 2:5). And blessed be God, Christ agreed to accomplish that atonement by the initiation of His Father and did accomplish it with His full approbation (Ps. 40:7–8; Mark 15:37–39). "For he hath made him to be sin for us, who knew no sin; that we might be made the righteousness of God in him" (2 Cor. 5:21). As the Dutch Reformed form for the Lord's Supper states, "The wrath of God against sin is so great, that (rather than it should go unpunished) He hath punished the same in His beloved Son Jesus Christ with the bitter and shameful death of the cross."[10]

By free grace, God regenerates sinners and causes them to believe in Christ alone as their righteousness and salvation. Those of us who are among these blessed believers are also made partakers of Christ's holiness by means of divine discipline (Heb. 12:10). As Christ's disciples, we are called by God to be more holy than we shall ever become by ourselves during this life (1 John 1:10).[11] He calls us to separate from sin and to consecrate and assimilate ourselves to Himself out of gratitude for His great salvation. These concepts—separation from sin, consecration to God, and conformity to Christ—make holiness comprehensive. Everything, Paul tells us in 1 Timothy 4:4–5, is to be sanctified, that is, made holy.

In the first place, personal holiness demands personal wholeness. God never calls us to give Him only a piece of our hearts. The call to holiness is a call for our entire heart: "My son, give me thine heart" (Prov. 23:26).

Second, holiness of heart must be cultivated in every sphere of life: in privacy with God, in the confidentiality of our homes, in the competitiveness of our occupation, in the pleasures of social friendship, in relation with our unevangelized neighbors and the world's hungry and unemployed, as well as in Sunday worship. Horatius Bonar writes:

> Holiness . . . extends to every part of our persons, fills up our being, spreads over our life, influences everything we are, or do, or think, or speak, or plan, small or great, outward or inward, negative or positive, our loving, our hating, our sorrowing, our rejoicing, our recreations, our business, our friendships, our relationships, our silence, our speech, our reading, our writing, our going out and our coming in—our whole man in every movement of spirit, soul, and body.[12]

Answering the call to holiness is a daily task. It is an absolute, radical call involving the core of religious faith and practice. John Calvin put it this way: "Because they have been called to holiness, the entire life of all Christians must be an exercise in piety."[13] In short, the call to holiness is a whole-life commitment to live "God-ward" (2 Cor. 3:4), to be set apart to the lordship of Jesus Christ.

Thus, holiness must be inward, filling our entire heart, and outward, covering all of life. "And the very God of peace sanctify you wholly; and I pray God your whole spirit and soul and body be preserved blameless unto the coming of our Lord Jesus Christ" (1 Thess. 5:23). "Holiness," Thomas Boston maintained, "is a constellation of graces."[14] In gratitude to God, a believer cultivates the fruits of holiness, such as meekness, gentleness, love, joy, peace, patience, kindness, goodness, mercy, contentment, gratitude, purity of heart, faithfulness, the fear of God, humility, spiritual-mindedness, self-control, and self-denial (Gal. 5:22–23).[15]

This call to holiness is not a call to merit acceptance with God. The New Testament declares that every believer is sanctified by the sacrifice of Christ: "By the which will we are sanctified through the offering of the body of Jesus Christ once for all" (Heb. 10:10). Christ is our sanctification (1 Cor. 1:30); therefore, the church, as the bride of Christ, is sanctified (Eph. 5:25–26). The believer's *status* before God is one of sanctity in Christ, on account of His perfect obedience which has fully satisfied the justice of God for all sin.

The believer's status, however, does not imply that he has arrived at a wholly sanctified *condition* (1 Cor. 1:2). Several attempts have been made to express the relationship between the believer's status and his condition before God, foremost among them being Luther's well-known *simul justus et peccator* ("at once righteous and a sinner"). That is to say, the believer is both righteous in God's sight because of Christ and remains a sinner as measured according to his own merits.[16] Though from the onset of Christian experience (which coincides with regeneration) the believer's status makes an impact on his condition, he is never in a perfectly sanctified condition in this life. Paul prays that the Thessalonians may be sanctified wholly, something that still has to be accomplished (1 Thess. 5:23). Sanctification received is sanctification well and truly begun, though not yet sanctification perfected.

This explains the New Testament's emphasis on holiness as something to be cultivated and pursued. New Testament language stresses vital, progressive sanctification. The believer must strive for sanctity, for holiness (Heb. 12:14). Growth in holiness must and will follow regeneration (Eph. 1:4; Phil. 3:12).

Thus, true believer, holiness is both something you have before God in Christ and something you must cultivate in the strength of Christ. Your status in holiness is conferred; your condition in holiness must be pursued. Through Christ you are made holy in your standing before God, and through Christ you are called to reflect that standing by being holy in daily life. Your context of holiness is justification through Christ; and your route of holiness is to be crucified and resurrected with Him, which involves the continual "mortification of the old, and the quickening of the new man" (*Heidelberg Catechism*, Question 88). You are called to be in life what you already are in principle by grace.

Concretely, then, what must you cultivate? (1) Imitation of the character of Jehovah; (2) conformity to the image of Christ; and (3) submission to the Holy Spirit.

Imitation of the Character of Jehovah

God says, "Be ye holy; for I am holy" (1 Peter 1:16). The holiness of God Himself ought to be our foremost stimulus to cultivate holy living. Seek to be like your heavenly Father in righteousness, holiness, and integrity. In the Spirit, strive to think God's thoughts after Him via His Word, to be of one mind with Him, to live and act as God Himself would have you do.[17] As Stephen Charnock concludes: "This is the prime way of honouring God. We do not so glorify God by elevated admirations, or eloquent expressions, or pompous services for him, as when we aspire to a conversing with him with unstained spirits, and live *to* him in living *like* him."[18]

Conformity to the Image of Christ

Conformity to Christ is a favorite Pauline theme, of which one example must suffice: "Let this mind be in you, which was also in Christ Jesus: Who . . . made himself of no reputation, and took upon him the form of a servant . . . and . . . humbled himself, and became obedient unto death, even the death of the cross" (Phil. 2:5–8). Christ was humble, willing to give up His rights in order to obey God and serve sinners. If you would be holy, Paul is saying, be like-minded.

Do not aim for conformity to Christ as a condition of salvation, however, but as a fruit of salvation received by faith. We must look to Christ for holiness, for He is the fount and path of holiness. Seek no other path. Follow the advice of Augustine who contended that it is better to limp on the path than to run outside of it.[19] Do as Calvin taught: Set Christ before you as the mirror of sanctification, and seek grace to mirror Him in His image.[20] Ask in each situation encountered: "What would Christ think, say, and do?" Then trust Him for holiness. He will not disappoint you (James 1:2–7).

There is unending room for growth in holiness because Jesus is the bottomless well of salvation. You cannot go to Him too much for holiness, for He is holiness *par excellence*. He lived holiness; He merited holiness; He sends His Spirit to apply holiness. "Christ is all, and in all" (Col. 3:11)—holiness inclusive. As Luther profoundly set forth, "We in Christ = justification; Christ in us = sanctification."[21]

Submission to the Mind of the Holy Spirit

In Romans 8:6 Paul divides people into two categories— those who let themselves be controlled by their sinful natures (i.e., the carnally minded who follow fleshly desires) and those who follow after the Spirit (i.e., those who *mind* "the things of the Spirit," Rom. 8:5).

The Holy Spirit was sent to bring the believer's mind into submission to His mind (1 Cor. 2). He was given to make sinners holy; the most holy increasingly bow as willing servants under His control. Let us beg for grace to be willing servants more fully and more consistently.

How does the Spirit work this holy grace of submission to His mind, thereby making us holy?

- He shows us our need for holiness through conviction of sin, righteousness, and judgment (John 16:8).
- He implants the desire for holiness. His saving work never leads to despair but always to sanctification in Christ.
- He grants Christlikeness in holiness. He works upon our whole nature, molding us after Christ's image.
- He provides strength to live a holy life by indwelling and influencing our soul. If we live by the Spirit, we will not gratify the desires of our sinful nature (Gal. 5:16); rather, we will live in obedience to and dependence on the Spirit.

- Through our humble feeding on Scripture and the exercise of prayer, the Spirit teaches us His mind and establishes an ongoing realization that holiness remains essential to being worthy of God and His kingdom (1 Thess. 2:12; Eph. 4:1) and fit for His service (1 Cor. 9:24–25; Phil. 3:13).

Ephesians 5:18 says, "Be not drunk with wine, wherein is excess; but be filled with the Spirit." Thomas Watson comments: "The Spirit stamps the impression of his own sanctity upon the heart, as the seal prints its likeness upon the wax. The Spirit of God in a man perfumes him with holiness, and makes his heart a map of heaven."[22]

HOW TO CULTIVATE HOLINESS

*T*hat believers are called to holiness is indisputably clear. But the cardinal question remains: How does the believer cultivate holiness? Here are seven directions to assist us.

1. Know and Love Scripture

Scripture is God's primary road to holiness and to spiritual growth—with the Spirit as Master Teacher blessing the reading and searching of God's Word. Jesus prayed, "Sanctify them through thy truth: thy word is truth" (John 17:17). And Peter advised, "Desire the sincere milk of the word, that ye may grow thereby" (1 Peter 2:2).

If you would not remain spiritually ignorant and impoverished, read through the Bible at least annually. Even more importantly, memorize the Scriptures (Ps. 119:11), search (John 5:39) and meditate upon them (Ps. 1:2), live and love them (Ps. 119; 19:10). Compare Scripture with Scripture; take time to study the Word. Proverbs 2:1–5 sets before us the principles of serious personal Bible study: teachability (receiving God's words), obedience (storing God's commandments), discipline (applying the heart), dependence (crying for knowledge), and perseverance (searching for hidden treasure).[1] Do not expect growth in holiness if you spend little time alone with God and do not take His Word seriously. When you are plagued with a heart prone to be tempted away from holiness, let Scripture teach you how to live a holy life in an unholy world.

Develop a scriptural formula for holy living. Here is one possibility drawn from 1 Corinthians. When hesitant over a course of action, ask yourself:

- Does this glorify God? (1 Cor. 10:31)
- Is this consistent with the lordship of Christ? (1 Cor. 7:23)
- Is this consistent with biblical examples? (1 Cor. 11:1)
- Is this lawful and beneficial for me—spiritually, mentally, physically? (1 Cor. 6:9–12)
- Does this help others positively and not hurt others unnecessarily? (1 Cor. 10:33; 8:13)
- Does this bring me under any enslaving power? (1 Cor. 6:12)

Let Scripture be your compass to guide you in cultivating holiness, in making life's decisions, and in encountering the high waves of personal affliction.

2. Use the Sacraments to Strengthen Faith

Use the sacraments of baptism and the Lord's Supper diligently as means of grace to strengthen your faith in Christ. God's sacraments complement His Word. They point us away from ourselves. Each sign—the water, the bread, the wine—directs us to believe in Christ and His sacrifice on the cross. The sacraments are visible means through which He invisibly communes with us and we with Him. They are spurs to Christlikeness and therefore to holiness.

Grace received through the sacraments is not different from that received through the Word. Both convey the same Christ. But as Robert Bruce put it, "While we do not get a better Christ in the sacraments than we do in the Word, there are times when we get Christ better."[2]

Flee often to Christ by Word and sacrament. Faith in Christ is a powerful motivator for holiness, since faith and the love of sin cannot mix. Be careful, however, not to seek your holiness in your experiences of Christ, but in Christ Himself. As William Gurnall admonishes:

> When thou trustest in Christ *within* thee, instead of Christ *without* thee, thou settest Christ against Christ. The bride does well to esteem her husband's picture, but it were ridiculous if she should love it better than himself, much more if she should go to it *rather than to him to supply her wants*. Yet thou actest thus when thou art more fond of Christ's image in thy soul than of him who painted it there.[3]

3. Be Dead to Sin, Alive in Christ

Regard yourself as dead to the dominion of sin and as alive to God in Christ (Rom. 6:11). "To realize this," writes Martyn

Lloyd-Jones, "takes away from us that old sense of hopelessness which we have all known and felt because of the terrible power of sin. . . . I can say to myself that not only am I no longer under the dominion of sin, but I am under the dominion of another power that nothing can frustrate."[4] That does not imply that because sin no longer reigns over us as believers, we have license to forgo our duty to fight against sin. Jerry Bridges rightly admonishes us, "To confuse the *potential* for resisting sin (which God provided) with the *responsibility* for resisting (which is ours) is to court disaster in our pursuit of holiness."[5] Westminster's Shorter Catechism balances God's gift and our responsibility when stating, "Sanctification is the work of God's free grace, whereby we are renewed in the whole man after the image of God, and are enabled more and more to die unto sin, and live unto righteousness" (Question 35).

Seek to cultivate a growing hatred of sin *as sin*, for that is the kind of hatred against sin that God possesses. Recognize that God is worthy of obedience not only as the Judge, but especially as a loving Father. Say with Joseph in temptation, "How then can I do this great wickedness, and sin against God?" (Gen. 39:9).

Look for heart-idols. Pray for strength to uproot them and cast them out. Attack all sin, all unrighteousness, and all devices of Satan.

Strive for daily repentance before God. Never rise above the publican's petition, "God be merciful to me a sinner" (Luke 18:13). Remember Luther's advice that God would have His people exercise "lifelong repentance."

Believe that Christ is mighty to preserve you alive by His Spirit. You live through union with Christ, therefore live unto His righteousness. His righteousness is greater than your unrighteousness. His Saviorhood is greater than your sinfulness. His Spirit is within you: "Ye are of God, little children, and have overcome [the false spirits]: because greater is he that is in you, than he that is in the world" (1 John 4:4). Do not despair: you are strong in Him, alive in Him, and victorious in Him. Satan may win many skirmishes, but the war is yours, the victory is yours (1 Cor. 15:57; Rom. 8:37). In Christ, the optimism of divine grace reigns over the pessimism of human nature.

4. Pray and Work

Pray and work in dependence upon God for holiness. No one but God is sufficient to bring a clean thing out of an unclean (Job 14:4). Hence, pray with David, "Create in me a clean heart, O God" (Ps. 51:10). And as you pray, work.

The Heidelberg Catechism (Question 116) points out that prayer and work belong together. They are like two oars, which when both are utilized, will keep a rowboat moving forward. If you use only one oar—if you pray without working or you work without praying—you will row in circles.

Holiness and prayer have much in common. Both are central to the Christian life and faith; they are obligatory, not optional. Both originate with God and focus upon Him. Both are activated, often simultaneously, by the Spirit of God. Neither can survive without the other. Both are learned by experience and through spiritual battles.[6] Neither is perfected in this life, but must be cultivated lifelong. Both are easier to talk and write about than to exercise. The most prayerful often feel themselves to be prayerless; the most holy often regard themselves as unholy.

Holiness and work are also closely related, especially the work of nurturing and persevering in *personal discipline*. Discipline takes time and effort. Paul exhorted Timothy, "Exercise thyself rather unto godliness" (1 Tim. 4:7). Holiness is not achieved sloppily or instantaneously.[7] Holiness is a call to a disciplined life; it cannot live out of what Dietrich Bonhoeffer called cheap grace—that is, grace which forgives without demanding repentance and obedience. Holiness is costly grace—grace that cost God the blood of His Son, cost the Son His own life, and costs the believer daily mortification so that, with Paul, he dies daily (1 Cor. 15:31).[8] Gracious holiness calls for continual commitment, continual diligence, continual practice, and continual repentance.[9] "If we sometimes through weakness fall into sin, we must not therefore despair of God's mercy, nor continue in sin, since . . . we have an eternal covenant of grace with God."[10] Rather, resolve with Jonathan Edwards: "Never to give over, nor in the least to slacken, my fight with my corruptions, however unsuccessful I may be."[11]

These two things, *fighting against sin* and *lack of success*, appear contradictory but are not. Failing and becoming a failure are two different matters. The believer recognizes he will often fail. Luther said that the righteous man feels himself more often to be "a loser than a victor" in the struggle against sin, "for the Lord lets him be tested and assailed to his utmost limits as gold is tested in a furnace."[12] This too is an important component of discipleship. Nevertheless, the godly man will persevere even through his failures. Failure does not make him quit; it makes him repent the more earnestly and press on in the Spirit's strength. "For a just man falleth seven times, and riseth up again: but the wicked shall fall into mischief" (Prov. 24:16). As John Owen wrote, "God works in us and with us, not against us or without us; so that his assistance is an encouragement as to the facilitating of the work, and no occasion of neglect as to the work itself."[13]

Let us never forget that the God we love, loves holiness. Hence the intensity of His fatherly, chastising discipline (Heb. 12:5–6, 10)! Perhaps William Gurnall says it best: "God would not rub so hard if it were not to fetch out the dirt that is ingrained in our natures. God loves purity so well He had rather see a hole than a spot in his child's garments."[14]

5. Flee Worldliness

We must strike out against the first appearance of the pride of life, the lusts of the flesh and eye, and all forms of sinful worldliness as they knock on the door of our hearts and minds. If we open the door and allow them to roam about in our minds and take foothold in our lives, we are already their prey. "Daniel purposed *in his heart* that he would not defile himself with the portion of the king's meat, nor with the wine which he drank: *therefore* he requested of the prince of the eunuchs that he might not defile himself" (Dan. 1:8; emphasis added). The material we read, the recreation and entertainment we engage in, the music we listen to, the friendships we form, and the conversations we have all affect our minds and ought to be judged in the context of Philippians 4:8: Whatsoever things are true, honest, just, pure, lovely, and of good report, "think on these things." We must live *above* the world and not be *of* the world while yet *in* the world (Rom. 12:1–2). If you stand *on* the Word, you will not stand *with* the world.

6. Seek Fellowship in the Church

Associate with mentors in holiness (Eph. 4:12–13; 1 Cor. 11:1).[15] The church ought to be a fellowship of mutual care and a community of prayer (1 Cor. 12:7; Acts 2:42). Converse and pray with fellow believers whose godly walk you admire (Col. 3:16). "He that walketh with the wise shall be wise" (Prov. 13:20). Association promotes assimilation. A Christian life lived in isolation from other believers will be defective; usually such a believer will remain spiritually immature. We cannot have a *heavenly* fellowship if we promote a *hindering* fellowship.

Such conversation, however, ought not to exclude the reading of godly treatises of former ages which promote holiness.

Luther said that some of his best friends were dead ones. For example, he questioned if anyone could possess spiritual life who did not feel kinship with David pouring out his heart in the Psalms. Read classics that speak out vehemently against sin. Let Thomas Watson be your mentor in *The Mischief of Sin*; John Owen, in *Temptation and Sin*; Jeremiah Burroughs, in *The Evil of Evils*; Ralph Venning, in *The Plague of Plagues*.[16] But also read J. C. Ryle's *Holiness*, Octavius Winslow's *Personal Declension and Revival of Religion in the Soul*, and John Flavel's *Keeping the Heart*.[17] Let these divines of former ages become your spiritual mentors and friends.

7. Commit Completely to God

Live present-tense, total commitment to God. Form habits of holiness. Pursue harmony and symmetry in holy living. Root out all inconsistencies, by the grace of the Spirit, and enjoy godly activities. Be committed to not get dirty with this world's temptations and to remain clean by forgiveness from and consecration to your perfect Savior.

Don't fall prey to the "one-more-time" syndrome. Postponed obedience is disobedience. Tomorrow's holiness is impurity *now*. Tomorrow's faith is unbelief *now*. Aim not to sin at all (1 John 2:1); ask for divine strength to bring every thought into captivity to Christ (2 Cor. 10:5), for Scripture indicates that our "thought-lives" ultimately determine our character: "For as he thinketh in his heart, so is he" (Prov. 23:7a). An old proverb says it this way:

> Sow a thought, reap an act;
> Sow an act, reap a habit;
> Sow a habit, reap a character;
> Sow a character, reap a destiny.

10

ENCOURAGEMENTS FOR CULTIVATING HOLINESS

The cultivation of holiness is demanding. Thomas Watson called it "sweating work." Happily, God provides us with several motives to holiness in His Word. To encourage us in the pursuit of holiness, we need to keep our eyes focused on the following biblical truths.

God Has Called Us to Holiness

"For God hath not called us unto uncleanness, but unto holiness" (1 Thess. 4:7). Whatever God calls us to is necessary. His call itself, as well as the benefits which we experience from holy living, should induce us to seek and practice holiness.

Holiness augments our spiritual well-being. God assures us that "no good thing will he withhold from them that walk

94

uprightly" (Ps. 84:11). "What health is to the heart," John
Flavel noted, "that holiness is to the soul."[1] In Richard Baxter's work on holiness, the very chapter titles are enlightening:
"Holiness is the only way of safety. Holiness is the only honest way. Holiness is the most gainful way. Holiness is the most
honourable way. Holiness is the most pleasant way."[2]

But most importantly, holiness glorifies the God you love
(Isa. 43:21). As Thomas Brooks affirmed, "Holiness makes
most for God's honour."[3]

Holiness Fosters Christlikeness

Thomas Watson wrote: "We must endeavour to be like
God in sanctity. It is a clear glass in which we can see a face;
it is a holy heart in which something of God can be seen."[4]
Christ serves here as a pattern of holiness for us—a pattern
of holy humility (Phil. 2:5–13), holy compassion (Mark 1:41),
holy forgiveness (Col. 3:13), holy unselfishness (Rom. 15:3),
holy indignation against sin (Matt. 23), and holy prayer (Heb.
5:7). Cultivated holiness which resembles God and is pat-
terned after Christ saves us from much hypocrisy and from
resorting to a "Sunday only" Christianity. It gives vitality,
purpose, meaning, and direction to daily living.

Holiness Gives Evidence of Justification and Election

Sanctification is the inevitable fruit of justification (1 Cor.
6:11). The two may be distinguished, but never separated; God
Himself has married them. Justification is organically linked
to sanctification; new birth infallibly issues in new life. The
justified will walk in "the King's highway of holiness."[5] In and
through Christ, justification gives God's child the *title* for
heaven and the boldness to enter; sanctification gives him the

fitness for heaven and the preparation necessary to enjoy it. Sanctification is the personal appropriation of the fruits of justification. B. B. Warfield notes, "Sanctification is but the execution of the justifying decree. For it to fail would be for the acquitted person not to be released in accordance with his acquittal."[6] Consequently, the justifying decree of Christ in John 8, "Neither do I condemn thee," is immediately followed by the call to holiness, "Go, and sin no more" (v. 11).

Election is also inseparable from holiness: "God hath from the beginning chosen you to salvation through sanctification of the Spirit" (2 Thess. 2:13). Sanctification is the earmark of Christ's elect sheep. That is why election is always a comforting doctrine for the believer, for it is the sure foundation that explains the grace of God working within him. No wonder our Reformed forebears deemed election to be one of the believer's greatest comforts, for sanctification visualizes election.[7]

Calvin insisted that election should discourage none, for the believer receives comfort from it, and the unbeliever is not called to consider it—rather, he is called to repentance. Whoever is discouraged by election or relies upon election without living a holy life is falling prey to a satanic misuse of this precious, encouraging doctrine (see Deut. 29:29). As J. C. Ryle asserts, "It is not given to us in this world to study the pages of the book of life, and see if our names are there. But if there is one thing clearly and plainly laid down about election, it is this—that elect men and women may be known and distinguished by holy lives."[8] Holiness is the visible side of their salvation. "Ye shall know them by their fruits" (Matt. 7:16).

Holiness Promotes Assurance (1 John 2:3; 3:19)

"Everyone may be assured in himself of his faith by the fruits thereof" (*Heidelberg Catechism*, Question 86). Reformed divines agree that most of the forms and degrees of assurance experienced by true believers—especially daily assurance—are reached gradually in the path of sanctification through careful cultivation of God's Word, the means of grace, and corresponding obedience.[9] An increasing hatred of sin, by means of mortification, and a growing love to obey God, by means of vivification, accompany the progress of faith as it grows into assurance. Christ-centered, Spirit-worked holiness is the best and most sound evidence of divine sonship (Rom. 8:1–16).

The way to lose a daily sense of assurance is to forgo the daily pursuit of holiness. Many believers live too carelessly. They treat sin lightly or neglect daily devotions and study of the Word. Others live too inactively. They do not cultivate holiness, but assume the posture that nothing can be done to foster sanctification, as if holiness were something *outside* of us except on rare occasions when something very special "happens" *inside*. To live carelessly or inactively is to ask for daily spiritual darkness, deadness, and fruitlessness.

Holiness Purifies Us

"Unto the pure all things are pure: but unto them that are defiled and unbelieving is nothing pure" (Titus 1:15). Holiness cannot be exercised where the heart has not been fundamentally transformed through divine regeneration. Through the new birth, Satan is deposed, the law of God is written upon the heart of the believer, Christ is crowned Lord and King, and the believer made "willing and ready, henceforth, to live unto Him" (*Heidelberg Catechism*, Question 1). Christ in us *(Christus in nobis)* is an essential complement to Christ for us *(Christus pro nobis)*.[10] The Spirit of God not only teaches the believer what Christ has done, but actualizes the holiness and work of Christ in his personal life. Through Christ, God sanctifies His child and makes his prayers and thanksgivings acceptable. As Thomas Watson said: "A holy heart is the altar which sanctifies the offering; if not to satisfaction, to acceptation."[11]

Holiness Is Essential for Effective Service to God

Paul joins sanctification and usefulness together: "If a man therefore purge himself from these, he shall be a vessel unto honour, sanctified and meet for the master's use, and prepared unto every good work" (2 Tim. 2:21). God uses holiness to assist the preaching of the gospel, to build up the credit of the Christian faith, which is dishonored by the carelessness of Christians and hypocrites who often serve as Satan's best allies.[12] Our lives are always doing good or harm; they are an open epistle for all to read (2 Cor. 3:2). Holy living influences and impresses as nothing else can; no argument can match it. It displays the beauty of religion; it gives credibility to witness and to evangelism (Phil. 2:15).[13] "Holiness," writes Hugh Morgan, "is the most effective way of influencing unconverted people and creating within them a willingness to listen to the preaching of the gospel" (Matt. 5:16; 1 Peter 3:1–2).[14]

Holiness manifests itself in humility and reverence for God. Such are those whom God looks to and uses (Isa. 66:2). As Andrew Murray notes:

> The great test of whether the holiness we profess to seek or to attain is truth and life will be *whether it be manifest in the increasing humility it produces*. In the creature, humility is the one thing needed to allow God's holiness to dwell in him and shine through him. In Jesus, the holy one of God who makes us holy, a divine humility was the secret of his life and his death and his exaltation; the one infallible test of our holiness will be the

humility before God and men which marks us. Humility is the bloom and the beauty of holiness.[15]

Holiness Fits Us for Heaven (Rev. 21:27)

Hebrews 12:14 says, "Follow [literally: *pursue*]. . . holiness, without which no man shall see the Lord." As John Owen wrote:

> There is no imagination wherewith man is besotted, more foolish, none so pernicious, as this—that persons not purified, not sanctified, not made holy in their life, should afterwards be taken into that state of blessedness which consists in the enjoyment of God. Neither can such persons enjoy God, nor would God be a reward to them. Holiness indeed is perfected in heaven: but the beginning of it is invariably confined to this world. God leads none to heaven but whom He sanctifies on the earth. This living Head will not admit of dead members.[16]

Holiness and worldliness, therefore, are antithetical to each other. If we're caught up with this world, we are not ready for the next.

11

OBSTACLES TO
CULTIVATING HOLINESS

*T*he cultivation of holiness will inevitably meet with numerous obstacles. Much impedes holiness. There are five common problems against which we need to be on guard.

Self-Centeredness

Our attitude toward sin and life itself is prone to be more self-centered than God-centered. We are often more concerned about the consequences of sin or victory over sin than about how our sins grieve God. The cultivation of holiness necessitates hating sin as God hates sin. Holiness is not merely loving God and our neighbor; it also involves hatred. The hatred of sin is of the essence of holiness. Those who love God hate sin (Prov. 8:36). We must cultivate an attitude that views sin as always being preeminently against God (Ps. 51:4).[1]

Distorted views of sin reap distorted views of holiness. "Wrong views about holiness are generally traceable to wrong views about human corruption," J. C. Ryle asserted. "If a man does not realize the dangerous nature of his soul's diseases, you cannot wonder if he is content with false or imperfect remedies."[2] Cultivating holiness demands a rejection of the pride of life and the lusts of the flesh. It also demands the prayer, "Give me the single eye, Thy Name to glorify" (Psalter 236, stanza 2).

We fail when we do not consciously live with our priorities centered on God's Word, will, and glory. In the words of the Scottish theologian John Brown, "Holiness does not consist in mystic speculations, enthusiastic fervours, or uncommanded austerities; it consists in thinking as God thinks, and willing as God wills."[3]

Neglect of Effort

Our progress is hindered when we misunderstand "living by faith" (Gal. 2:20) to imply that no effort toward holiness is commanded of us. Sometimes we are even prone to consider human effort sinful or "fleshly." Bishop Ryle provides us with a corrective here:

> Is it wise to proclaim in so bald, naked, and unqualified a way as many do, that the holiness of converted people is by faith only, and not at all by personal exertion? Is this according to the proportion of God's Word? I doubt it. That faith in Christ is the root of all holiness no well-instructed Christian will ever think of denying. But surely the Scriptures teach us that in fol-

lowing holiness the true Christian needs personal exertion and work as well as faith.[4]

We are responsible for holiness. Whose fault is it but our own if we are not holy? As Ralph Erskine counsels, we need to implement the *fight-or-flight* attitude with regard to sinful temptations. Sometimes we simply need to heed Peter's plain injunction, "Dearly beloved, I beseech you as strangers and pilgrims, abstain from fleshly lusts, which war against the soul" (1 Peter 2:11). *Abstain*—often it is that simple.

If you have put off the old man and put on the new (Eph. 4:22–32), live accordingly (Col. 3:9–10). Mortify your members (i.e. unholy habits) and seek those things which are above (Col. 3:1–5)—not as a form of legalism, but as a repercussion of divine blessing (Col. 2:9–23).[5] Make a covenant with your eyes and feet and hands to turn from iniquity (Job 31:1). Look the other way; walk the other way. Put away uncontrolled anger, gossip, and bitterness. Put sin to death (Rom. 8:13) by the blood of Christ. "Set faith at work on Christ for the killing of thy sin," wrote John Owen, "and thou wilt . . . live to see thy lust dead at thy feet."[6]

Dependence on Our Own Efforts

On the other hand, we fail miserably when we take pride in our holiness and think that our exertions can somehow produce holiness apart from faith. From beginning to end holiness is the work of God and His free grace (*Westminster Confession of Faith*, ch. 13). As Richard Sibbes maintained, "By grace we are what we are in justification, and work what we work in sanctification."[7] Holiness is not partially God's work and partially our work. Holiness manufactured by our heart is not holiness after God's heart. All working out of the Christian life on our part is the fruit of God working in us and through us: "Work out your own salvation with fear and trembling. For it is God which worketh in you both to will and to do of his good pleasure" (Phil. 2:12–13).

"The regenerate have a spiritual nature within that fits them for holy action, otherwise there would be no difference between them and the unregenerate," wrote A. W. Pink.[8] Nevertheless, self-sanctification, strictly speaking, is nonexistent.[9] "We do good works, but not to merit by them (for what can we merit?), nay, we are beholden to God for the good works we do, and not He to us" (*Belgic Confession of Faith*, Article 24). As Calvin explained, "Holiness is not a merit by which we can attain communion with God, but a gift of Christ which enables us to cling to him and to follow him."[10] John Murray put it this way: "God's working in us is not suspended because we work, nor our working suspended because God works. Neither is the relation strictly one of cooperation as if God did his part and we did ours. . . . God works in us and we also work. But the relation is that *because* God works we work."[11]

> And every virtue we possess,
> And every conquest won,
> And every thought of holiness,
> Are His alone.

Kenneth Prior warns: "There is a subtle danger of speaking of sanctification as essentially coming from our own effort or initiative. We can unconsciously do this even while acknowledging our need for the power of the Holy Spirit, by making the operation of that power dependent upon our surrender and consecration."[12]

Our dependence on God for holiness ought to humble us. Holiness and humility are inseparable.[13] Of what they have in common, not least is that neither one recognizes itself. The

103

most holy complain of their impurity; the most humble, of their pride. Those of us who are called to be teachers and examples of holiness must beware of subtle and insidious pride working its way into our supposed holiness.

Holiness is greatly impeded by any number of wrong views of holiness in its relation to humility; for example:

- As soon as we think, speak, or act as if our own holiness will somehow suffice us without being clothed with Christ's humility, we are already enveloped by spiritual pride.
- When we begin to feel complacent about our holiness, we are far from both holiness and humility.
- When self-abasement is lacking, holiness is lacking.
- When self-abasement does not make us to flee to Christ and His holiness for refuge, holiness is lacking.
- Without a life dependent on Christ, we shall possess no holiness.

Erroneous Views about Holiness

Embracing unscriptural, erroneous views about holiness can greatly impede our holiness. The need to experience "the second blessing," an earnest search for our own special gift of the Spirit (or the desire to exercise a charismatic gift such as speaking in tongues or faith healing), and the acceptance of Jesus as Savior but not as Lord—these are but a few of the many erroneous interpretations of Scripture that can skew a proper understanding of biblical holiness in our personal lives.

Though addressing these issues lies beyond the scope of this chapter, allow me to provide three summary statements. Concerning the first error mentioned above, it is not just *the* second blessing that the believer needs, but he needs *a* second blessing, as well as a third and fourth and fifth—yes, he needs the continual blessing of the Holy Spirit in order to progress in holiness so that Christ may increase and he may decrease (John 3:30). Concerning the second error mentioned above, John Stott wisely comments that "when Paul wrote to the Corinthians that they were not lacking in spiritual gifts (1 Cor. 1:7), he makes it clear that the evidence of the Spirit's fullness is not the exercise of His gifts (of which they had plenty), but the ripening of His fruit (of which they had little)."[14] And with regard to the third error of separating the Savior from His lordship, the Heidelberg Catechism provides a summary corrective in Question 30: "One of these two things must be true, that either Jesus is not a complete Savior or that they, who by a true faith receive this Savior, must find all things in Him necessary to their salvation."

Avoidance of the Conflict

We are prone to shirk the battle of daily spiritual warfare. No one likes war. In addition, the believer is often blind to his real enemies—to a subtle Satan, to a tempting world, and especially to the reality of his own ongoing pollution which Paul so poignantly describes in Romans 7:14–25. To be holy among the holy takes grace; to be holy among the unholy is great grace. Maintaining personal holiness in an unholy world with a heart prone to backslide necessitates a perpetual fight. It will involve conflict, holy warfare, struggle against Satan, a battle between the flesh and the spirit (Gal. 5:17). A believer not only has peace of conscience, but also war within (Rom. 7:24–8:1). As Samuel Rutherford asserts, "The devil's war is better than the devil's peace."[15] Hence the remedies of Christ's holiness (Heb. 7:25–28) and of His Spirit-supplied Christian armor (Eph. 6:10–20) are ignored at our peril. True holiness must be pursued against the backdrop of an acute awareness of indwelling sin which continues to live in our hearts and to deceive our understanding. The holy man, unlike others, is never at peace with indwelling sin. Though he may backslide far, he will again be humbled and ashamed because of his sin.

THE JOY OF
CULTIVATING HOLINESS

A holy life ought to be one of joy in the Lord, not negative drudgery (Neh. 8:11). The idea that holiness requires a gloomy disposition is a tragic distortion of Scripture. On the contrary, Scripture asserts that those who cultivate holiness experience true joy. Jesus said, "If ye keep my commandments, ye shall abide in my love; even as I have kept my Father's commandments, and abide in his love. These things have I spoken unto you that your joy might remain in you, and that your joy might be full" (John 15:10–11). Those who are obedient—who are pursuing holiness as a way of life—will know that joy which flows from communion with God is a supreme joy, an ongoing joy, and an anticipated joy.

The Supreme Joy: Fellowship with God

No greater joy can be had than that of communion with God. "In thy presence is fulness of joy" (Ps. 16:11). True joy springs from God as we are enabled to walk in fellowship with Him. When we break our fellowship with God by sin, we need to return, like David, with penitential prayer to Him: "Restore unto me the joy of thy salvation" (Ps. 51:12). The words Jesus spoke to the thief on the cross represent the chief delight of every child of God: "Today shalt thou be with me in paradise" (Luke 23:43).

The Ongoing Joy: Abiding Assurance

True holiness obeys God, and obedience always trusts God. It believes, "And we know that all things work together for good to them that love God" (Rom. 8:28)—even when it cannot be seen. Like faithful workers on a Persian carpet, who blindly hand up all colors of strand to the overseer working out the pattern above them, God's intimate saints are those who hand Him even the black strands He calls for, knowing that His pattern will be perfect from above, notwithstanding the gnarled mess underneath. Do you too know this profound, childlike trust in believing the words of Jesus: "What I do thou knowest not now: but thou shalt know hereafter" (John 13:7)? Such ongoing, stabilizing joy surpasses understanding. Holiness reaps joyous contentment; "godliness with contentment is great gain" (1 Tim. 6:6).

The Anticipated Joy: Eternal, Gracious Reward

Jesus was motivated to endure His sufferings by anticipating the joy of His reward (Heb. 12:1–2). Believers too may look forward to entering into the joy of their Lord as they pursue holiness in the strength of Christ throughout their lives. By grace, they may joyously anticipate their eternal reward: "Well done, thou good and faithful servant: . . . Enter thou into the joy of thy Lord" (Matt. 25:21, 23). As John Whitlock noted: "Here is the Christian's way and his end—his way is holiness, his end, happiness."[1]

Holiness is its own reward, for everlasting glory is holiness perfected. "The souls of believers are at their death made perfect in holiness" (*Westminster Shorter Catechism*, Question 37). Also their bodies shall be raised immortal and incorruptible, perfect in holiness, complete in glorification (1 Cor. 15:49, 53). Finally the believer shall be what he has desired to become ever since his regeneration—perfectly holy in a Triune God. He shall enter into the eternal glory of Jesus Christ as a son of God and fellow-heir with Him (Phil. 3:20–21; Rom. 8:17). He shall finally be like Christ, holy and without blemish (Eph. 5:25–27), eternally magnifying and exalting the unfathomable bounties of God's sovereign grace. Truly, as Calvin stated, "the thought of the great nobility God has conferred upon us ought to whet our desire for holiness."[2]

Cultivating Holiness as a Constant Struggle

I once read of a missionary who had in his garden a shrub that bore poisonous leaves. He also had a child who was prone to put anything within reach into his mouth. Naturally, the father dug the shrub out and threw it away. The shrub's roots, however, went very deep. Soon the shrub sprouted again. Repeatedly, the missionary had to dig it out. There was no solution but to inspect the ground every day and to dig up the shrub every time it surfaced. Indwelling sin is like that shrub. It needs constant uprooting. Our hearts need continual mortification. As John Owen warns us:

> We must be exercising [mortification] every day, and in every duty. Sin will not die, unless it be constantly weakened. Spare it, and it will heal its wounds, and recover its strength. We must continually watch against the operations of this principle of sin: in our duties, in our calling, in conversation, in retirement, in our straits, in our enjoyments, and in all that we do. If we are negligent on any occasion, we shall suffer by it; every mistake, every neglect is perilous.[3]

Press on in the uprooting of sin and the cultivation of holiness. Continue to fight the good fight of faith under the best of generals, *Jesus Christ*; with the best of internal advocates, *the Holy Spirit*; by the best of assurances, *the promises of God*; for the best of results, *everlasting glory*.

Have you been persuaded that cultivating holiness is worth the price of saying no to sin and yes to God? Do you know the joy of walking in God's ways? The joy of experiencing Jesus' easy yoke and light burden? The joy of not belonging to yourself, but belonging to your "faithful Savior Jesus Christ," who makes you "sincerely willing and ready, henceforth, to live unto Him" (*Heidelberg Catechism*, Question 1)? Are you holy? Thomas Brooks gives us sixteen marks of real holiness, including the holy believer "admires the holiness of God, . . . possesses diffusive holiness that spreads itself over head and heart, lip and life, inside and outside, . . . stretches himself after higher degrees of holiness, . . . hates and detests all ungodliness and wickedness, . . . grieves over his own vileness and unholiness."[4] It is a daunting list, yet a biblical one. No doubt we all fall far short, but the question remains: Are we striving for these marks of holiness?

Perhaps you respond, "Who is sufficient for these things?" (2 Cor. 2:16). Paul's ready answer is, "Not that we are sufficient of ourselves to think any thing as of ourselves; but our sufficiency is of God" (2 Cor. 3:5). "Would you be holy? . . . Then you must *begin with Christ*. . . . Would you continue holy? Then *abide in Christ*."⁵ "Holiness is not the way to Christ; Christ is the way of holiness."⁶ Outside of Christ there is no holiness. Then every list of the marks of holiness must condemn us to hell. Ultimately, of course, holiness is not a list; it is much more—it is a life, a life in Jesus Christ. Holiness in believers proves that they are joined to Christ, for sanctified obedience is impossible without Him. But in Christ the call to holiness remains within the context of *sola gratia* (by grace alone) and *sola fide* (by faith alone).⁷ "If thou, LORD, shouldest mark iniquities, O Lord, who shall stand? But there is forgiveness with thee, that thou mayest be feared" (Ps. 130:3–4).

"Since Christ cannot be known apart from the sanctification of the Spirit," Calvin writes, "it follows that faith can in no wise be separated from a devout disposition."⁸ Christ, the Holy Spirit, the Word of God, holiness, grace, and faith are inseparable. Make this your prayer: "Lord, grant that I might cultivate holiness today—not out of merit, but out of gratitude, by Thy grace through faith in Christ Jesus. Sanctify me by the blood of Christ, the Spirit of Christ, and the Word of God." Pray with Robert Murray M'Cheyne, "Lord, make me as holy as a pardoned sinner can be."⁹

PART 4

OVERCOMING
THE
WORLD
IN THE
MINISTRY

YOUR PRIVATE LIFE

aul's farewell message to the Ephesian elders is affectionate, yet full of solemn warning. Acts 20:28 is the heart of that message, and shows how we ministers must overcome worldliness in our work. Acts 20:28 says, "Take heed therefore unto yourselves, and to all the flock, over the which the Holy Ghost hath made you overseers, to feed the church of God, which he hath purchased with his own blood."

Paul gives three directives to consider as we battle worldliness in the ministry: (1) take heed to yourselves, (2) take heed to your flock, and (3) feed the church of God. He enforces each mandate with persuasions to persevere in our work, and to overcome the world. "Take heed," Paul says. Stop whatever you are doing. Pay close attention. Deny yourself, and consider what I say, for it is most important. Paul addresses the Ephesian elders much as we speak to young children. When we have something important to tell them, we bring them close, hold their heads in our hands, look into their eyes, and say, "Listen to me. This is very important."

We must "take heed" if we would fight against our tendency to be worldly. Our Savior used this very expression when He warned His disciples of the dangers of ministry: "Take heed to yourselves, lest at any time your hearts be overcharged with surfeiting, and drunkenness, and cares of this life, and so that day come upon you unawares" (Luke 21:34).

In this section of this book, we examine how we should "take heed" in our private life (ch. 13), our prayer life (ch. 14), our relationships with God (ch. 15) and our family (ch. 16), and our attitude to ministry as shown in how we fight against pride (ch. 17) and how we cope with criticism (ch. 18). Chapters 19 and 20 explore how we should take heed to our flock by being true to the official titles Scripture ascribes to us, with a special emphasis on our callings as preacher and shepherd. The concluding chapter provides a trinitarian framework, based on Acts 20:28, that serves as a powerful persuasion to overcome worldliness in the ministry.

Private Life Crucial to Public Life

Take heed to what you do in private. What a man is before God in private is what he truly is. Take heed, then, to what you are in the quietness of your study or in the solitude of your travel, when no one sees what you are doing. "We must have an inner life, out of which the outward life must flow," writes Philip Power. "The secret of an effective holy life in public, will ever prove to be a holy life with God in private; this is the root from which, in due season, will come both leaves and fruit."[1]

What you are in private counts more than what you are in public. That's why Paul habitually speaks of first taking heed to yourself. Personal godliness should go hand in hand with doctrinal purity. Thus, Paul writes to Timothy, "Take heed unto thyself, and unto the doctrine; continue in them: for in doing this thou shalt both save thyself, and them that hear thee" (1 Tim. 4:16).

How do we spend our private time? What prayers do we offer? What kind of relationship do we have with God?

The Development of Worldliness

Worldliness usually develops slowly in a minister, like a malignant cancer. It is often not detected until it is too late. The church in Ephesus was probably as shocked as anyone to hear that the Lord Jesus was grieved that she had left her first love (Rev. 2:4). Her head was correct in doctrine, her hands were busy in service, but her heart had become cold in affection. She was a backsliding church.

Worldliness and leaving our first love are Siamese twins. The tragic process of worldly backsliding usually begins in the inner closet of prayer. Our private intercessory prayers become cold, formal, and short. This backsliding then spreads to other parts of our ministry. Scripture becomes less relevant to us, preaching more laborious. Edifying literature loses its attraction.

As the Word of God loses its grip on us, inner corruptions multiply. Humility yields to pride. Communion with God dissipates. We begin to feel estranged from God. We start working *for* God rather than *with* Him. We still confess our sins and renew our vows, but our confession lacks genuine repentance, and our vows fail to yield genuine reformation. We examine ourselves less frequently, less thoroughly, less prayerfully.

Backsliding leads us to talk more *about* God than *to* God. Soon we also get presumptuous. We think we can endure trials and resist temptations in our own strength. "In my pros-

117

perity I said, I shall never be moved" (Ps. 30:6). We continue to think that way in spite of our failures and God's silence. Before long, we are living off past communion with God. We no longer feel the need to daily embrace Christ by faith. We feel little conviction of sin; rather, we become adept at justifying and rationalizing our weaknesses and shortcomings.

The line of separation between the godly and the ungodly becomes blurred. Somehow it seems easier to talk with worldly people about secular things than with believers about things of God. We become attracted to worldly amusements, such as television and secular literature. What we once considered frivolous—even dangerous—begins to take more of our time.

In the meantime, brotherly love for fellow Christians dissipates and becomes strained. We no longer love them enough to bear with their sinful tendencies. We lose perspective, and begin to argue over nonessentials. Molehills are made into mountains, and mountains are made into molehills. The fear of man crowds out the fear of God. We become irritable and impatient with problems in the congregation. We speak out against elders or deacons rather than privately dealing with their faults, with the result that the whole church suffers.

Our consciences become desensitized to Satan's devices. His power is no longer feared and his temptations are not strenuously resisted. We forget that Satan wants to have us, just as Jesus said Satan wanted to have Peter (Luke 22:31–32).

Ministers a Primary Target

Ministers are special objects of Satan's attention because of the office we hold. For the rest of our lives, we will be among Satan's primary targets. He will use every wile, and every weapon in his arsenal, to destroy our ministries and to discredit the gospel of Jesus Christ. As Calvin says, the ministry "is not an easy and indulgent exercise, but a hard and severe warfare, where Satan is exerting all his power against us, and moving every stone for our disturbance."[2] That ought to make us tremble, watch, and pray without ceasing. Satan works especially hard against us church leaders because of our past usefulness, our present position, and our potential value for the cause of Christ. As Baxter put it, "Satan knows what a rout he can make of the troops if he can make the leader fall before their eyes. If Satan can ensnare your feet, your hands, your tongue, and make you fall, your troops will scatter."[3]

Satan strategizes to attack us at our weakest points. We must therefore expect the most subtle temptations and the most violent assaults. How circumspect we must be! We must set a watch before every gate that leads into or out of our heart.[4] We must set a guard at every gate—at the gate of our imagination, our mind, and our hearts. We must take heed to our private thoughts before God. Like the psalmist, we must make sure that no wicked thing is set before our eyes (Ps. 101:3).

Perhaps one of the greatest dangers of worldliness that we face today comes through our eyes. Do you know that every year four thousand evangelical pastors become enmeshed in Internet pornography? Others think nothing of spending numerous hours watching television, or renting questionable videos to view at home. If you ask about the morality of what they watch, they'll probably say, "It isn't that bad." Sure, there's a bit of profanity. Some sex and violence, too. But "it really isn't that bad."

Ephesians 4:29–30 says, "Let no corrupt communication proceed out of your mouth, but that which is good to the use of edifying, that it may minister grace unto the hearers. And grieve not the holy Spirit of God, whereby ye are sealed unto the day of redemption." If you think that it grieves the Spirit of God for you to *speak* a corrupt word, why doesn't it grieve

119

the Spirit for you to *hear* a corrupt word? That *does* grieve Him.

There are times when we cannot avoid overhearing profanity used by others, but we do not need to invite it into our homes, and into our ears and minds and hearts. Take heed to what you do in private. Don't flirt with sin.

Consider the man who lived at the top of a mountain. He needed to hire someone to take his daughter up and down the mountain each day for school. So he interviewed various candidates, asking them, "How close can you come to the edge without going over?" The first man said, "I can come within twelve inches and not go over the edge." The second claimed, "I can come within six inches of the edge." The third boasted he could come within an inch. But the fourth said, "I don't know because I'll be hugging the other side. I will stay as far away from the edge as I can." You know who got the job.

Ways to Overcome Worldliness

Brothers, take warning. Stay away from the edge of worldliness. Recognize the danger! You and I are called to be examples to believers "in word, in conversation, in charity, in spirit, in faith, in purity" (1 Tim. 4:12). This does not happen automatically. The Spirit uses means to enable us to be examples— means rooted in our private lives. Here are a few of them:

- Take heed to God's Word, giving your attention "to reading, to exhortation, to doctrine" (v. 13), and to daily communing with God. As Thomas Boston wrote, "The most holy minister on earth, while he is feeding others with the one hand, hath need to put into his own mouth with the other." Richard Baxter added, "While we prepare the feast for others, we should not hesitate to lick our fingers." We must feed our own souls with the Word of God and keep Christ before our hearts if we would minister to others.

- Take heed to confess sin as soon as you are conscious of it. Psalm 36:9 says, "In thy light shall we see light." The Lord will not reveal His secrets to us when we do not dwell in the light of His favorable presence. The Puritans were fond of advising, "Keep short accounts with God." Only a habitually cleansed conscience will grant us the unclouded, uninterrupted communion with God we so desperately need in our private lives in order to pray to God for our church and to proclaim God's Word to His church.

- Take heed to keep your motives pure. Matthew 6:22 says, "The light of the body is the eye: if therefore thine eye be single, thy whole body shall be full of light." Do we have "the single eye, God's Name to glorify"?[5] You can't maintain the single-minded aim for God's glory if your vision and motives are sullied. Why did God often call Moses apart to spend time with Him? One reason surely was that the glory of God might remain Moses' overriding concern. This is God's goal with us in every cross we must carry. He afflicts us to keep us in close communion with Himself, to wean us from this world, and to ripen us for the eternal beatific vision of *soli Deo gloria*—in short, to keep us pure-minded, heavenly-minded!

Heaven must be in us before we are in heaven, as was said by Philip Henry, father of the commentator. Sitting in heavenly places together with Christ Jesus (Eph. 2:6) is the best cure for daily struggles with worldliness.

14

YOUR PRAYER LIFE

hy aren't ministers required to punch a clock or work a certain number of hours a week? It is because, according to Acts 6, the apostles set a precedent when they refused to take time away from preaching to do other things. Since to "leave the word of God, and serve tables" was not pleasing to Christ, who had commissioned them to preach, the apostles determined to give themselves "continually to prayer, and to the ministry of the word" (Acts 6:2, 4).

Note the order here: first prayer, then ministry. As Charles Bridges once wrote, "Prayer is one-half of our ministry; and it gives to the other half all its power and success."[1] Likewise, Jean Massillon (1663–1742), a French preacher, said to a group of ministers: "A pastor who does not pray, who does not love prayer, does not belong to that Church, which 'prays without ceasing.' He is a dry and barren tree, which cumbers the Lord's ground. He is the enemy, and not the father of his people."[2]

Our Failure to Pray

Our consciences may convict us here more than in any other part of ministry. You might never be careless in preparing sermons—in the hard work of exegesis or in the equally hard work of application—but you might have to hang your head in shame as you consider how little you have truly given yourself to prayer.

Part of our problem is that we view prayer as an appendix to our work rather than as the first major part of our work. If we are to live godly lives, we must pray. If we would learn the art of sacred wrestling and holy argument with God, we must pray. Prayer is the only way to lay hold of God. All the books we read on prayer and all the sermons we preach on prayer will be of no help unless we pray as Jacob did when he wrestled with God, saying, "I will not let thee go, except thou bless me" (Gen. 32:26).

Lack of prayer is the downfall of many ministers. Thomas Brooks once said, "A family without prayer is like a house without a roof, open and exposed to all the storms of heaven." Likewise, a pastor without prayer is like a church without a roof, open and exposed to all the storms of heaven, earth, and hell.

Prayer is diametrically opposed to worldliness, for worldliness looks no higher than this world. In essence, worldliness is a bid for independence from God. By contrast, prayer connects us with heaven. It expresses our dependence on God and begs for His guidance and blessing on everything we do. As John Owen says, "To preach the Word and not follow it with constant and fervent prayer for its success is to disbelieve its use, to neglect its end, and to cast away the seed of the gospel at random."

Wrestling with God in Prayer

If the giants of church history dwarf us today, perhaps it is not because they were more educated, more devout, or more faithful. Rather, it's because they were men of much prayer. They were Daniels in the temple of God. As Owen wrote, "A minister may fill his pews, his communion roll, and the mouths of the public, but what that minister is on his knees in secret before God Almighty, that he is and no more."

Take heed to your prayer life. As pastors, you are engaged in spiritual conflict over men's souls. That takes time, effort, energy, and much prayer. As Hudson Taylor aptly warned, "Do not be so busy with the work of Christ that you have no strength left for prayer."

Luther was a busy man at the helm of the Reformation, yet he prayed three hours daily. He once said to Melanchthon, "I must rise an hour early tomorrow, for, given all that I need to do, I must spend more time in prayer."

John Welsh, the son-in-law of John Knox, prayed seven hours a day. "I often wonder how a Christian could lie in his bed all night, and not rise to pray," he said. Welsh kept his robe at his bedside each night so he wouldn't catch cold when he rose to commune with God. Once his wife found him weeping after midnight and asked him what was wrong. "Oh my dear wife," he said, "I have 3,000 souls to answer for, and I know not how it is with many of them!" On another occasion, she overheard him pleading in broken sentences, "Lord, wilt Thou not grant me Scotland?"

Please don't misunderstand me. I'm not suggesting that we should try to spend seven hours a day praying. We would only be setting ourselves up for failure. The amount of time spent in prayer is not the main factor; genuine wrestling with God in prayer is far more important than the length of time spent in prayer. Yet can we as ministers accomplish our calling at the throne of grace each day in ten or fifteen minutes and still maintain an intimate life with the Lord? I seriously doubt that. If I claim to have an excellent marriage, but then tell you that I spend only fifteen minutes a day talking with my wife, what conclusion would you draw?

Serious wrestling at God's throne may not need hours of prayer on end, but it certainly cannot be accomplished on a habitual basis in a few minutes' worth of petitions. Our world desperately needs ministers who wrestle with God in prayer.

Let us refuse to relinquish the inner prayer chamber, for here the work of true reformation succeeds or fails. Refuse to be content with the shell of religion without the inner core of prayer. When we grow drowsy or sloppy in prayer, we should pray aloud, or write down our prayers, or find a quiet place outside to walk and pray. We must not stop praying.

Do not abandon stated times of prayer, but also pray when you feel the slightest impulse to do so. Conversing with God is the most effective way to ward off spiritual backsliding and discouragement. Discouragement without prayer is an open sore ripe for infection, whereas discouragement with prayer is an invitation for the balm of Gilead.

Keep prayer a priority in every part of your life. John Bunyan said, "Pray often, for prayer is a shield to the soul, a sacrifice to God, and a scourge to Satan." Pray before and after every church duty, be it preaching, calling on families, teaching catechism, or counseling a troubled couple.

Failing to "pray without ceasing" (1 Thess. 5:17) is the primary reason why there are so little unction and conviction in most preaching today. The problem is two-sided, to be sure. It is our fault as ministers because we too easily give up prayer

125

time, and it is the fault of our people when they make too many demands on us. Too many churches inadvertently pressure ministers to abandon prayer time by overloading their days with administrative duties, committee meetings, and counseling sessions. Many pastors today are busy studying the problems of the church and suggesting solutions, but where are the Daniels, Luthers, and Welshes who give themselves to prayer?

According to James 5:17 (KJV marginal note), Elijah "prayed in his prayer," displaying his intense devotion to this duty. We ought to be doing that as well. As Spurgeon wrote: "To you as the ambassadors of God, the mercy-seat has a virtue beyond all estimate. The more familiar you are with the court of heaven, the better shall you discharge your heavenly trust. . . . All our libraries and studies are mere emptiness compared with our closets. We grow, we are mighty, we prevail in private prayer."[3]

15

YOUR RELATIONSHIP
WITH GOD

The heartbeat of a godly life for any believer, but especially a pastor, is personal acquaintance with God. "Acquaint now thyself with him, and be at peace: thereby good shall come unto thee," Eliphaz says in Job 22:21. Someone who spends a day working with lilies in a greenhouse will end the day smelling like a lily. Likewise, a minister who spends his days communing with God and with Christ will preach sermons that are scented by that communion, with the "savour of his knowledge," the "sweet savour of Christ," and the "savour of life unto life" (2 Cor. 2:14–16).

Take heed to your relationship with God. Acquaintance with God will affect our entire ministry. It will influence us spiritually, intellectually, emotionally, and physically. Specifically, here is what's needed:

A Growing, Deep Acquaintance with God

Peter tells us to "grow in grace, and in the knowledge of our Lord and Saviour Jesus Christ" (2 Peter 3:18). And Paul says we must be changed by the Holy Spirit from one stage of glory to another (2 Cor. 3:18).

The implication is clear: spiritual life begins in the heart and is fueled by grace and knowledge. As our hearts are increasingly sanctified by God, our preaching will reflect that growth. We will be expressing the same eternal truths, but they will be enriched by various dimensions of our growing relationship with God. Though we speak of the same Father, the same Christ, the same Spirit, and the same covenant of grace that we spoke of years ago when we were first ordained into the ministry, those great themes will become richer and deeper as they are punctuated with the freshness of a growing relationship with God.

In a good marriage in which love grows and deepens, the partners remain the same but the relationship is never static. The relationship remains alive and dynamic as husband and wife grow in knowing, loving, and serving each other. If this is true between two finite personalities, how much more of a pastor's relationship with God, in which he explores the infinite depths of God's being and the glory of His salvation (Rom. 11:33).

Preaching is the mirror of a pastor's relationship with God. Woe to the minister whose congregation is lulled to sleep by stale and wooden messages from a pastor who is not growing in acquaintance with his Master.

A Varied Acquaintance with God

The Psalms show how varied the experience of knowing God and walking with Him is. Some people may expect the

Christian life to be continuous joy and victory. Triumph is reflected in some of the Psalms, but nearly half of them describe the pain, sorrow, frustration, and loneliness of Christian experience. We should look at all of the Psalms for a better understanding of what we will encounter in our walk with God. As Luther said, "If you can't find your life in the Psalms, you have never become a child of God."

Walking with God is a varied experience. A godly person may experience days of ecstatic joy and unspeakable peace, but those may be followed by days of struggle and pain. Likewise, pastors may have times when they praise God "with joyful lips" (Ps. 63:5) with David. But they may also have days when they cry out with Asaph, "Will the Lord cast off for ever? and will he be favourable no more? Is his mercy clean gone for ever? doth his promise fail for evermore? Hath God forgotten to be gracious? hath he in anger shut up his tender mercies?" (Ps. 77:7–9).

Preaching that does not incorporate large segments of the Word of God because the soul of the preacher is estranged from this varied experience of walking with God is one-sided, truncated, and narrow. Such preaching will not deeply satisfy exercised children of God. Paul understood the need for a complete understanding of the Christian's walk through life. Because he knew what anxiety was, he could teach believers how not to be anxious. Because he had personally battled fear and sin and disappointment, he could preach on those matters to other believers (2 Cor. 1:3–7).

A Unique Individual Acquaintance with God

Scripture speaks often of how God works in families, congregations, cities, and even nations. Yet believers are also individuals; no two leaves on a tree are precisely the same.

129

The purest, noblest form of individualism is taught in Scripture. For example, Jesus says, "The very hairs of your head are all numbered" (Matt. 10:30). That's astonishing individualism. He also says that He knows all of His sheep by name (John 10:3, 14). What is more individual than a person's name?

If our acquaintance with God is genuine, it must be original. We should not imitate the language or experience of another person but, in our own words, assert with John, "That which we have seen and heard declare we unto you" (1 John 1:3).

Walking with God is like crossing the ocean in a ship. One ship does not clear a path for another to follow. Each in turn must cross the same waters. In like manner each one of us must walk alone with God. We must trust God to sanctify us in every experience so that we become "able ministers of the new testament" (2 Cor. 3:6). God leads each one of us through experiences that are uniquely ordered to sanctify us. He leads us through afflictions, joys, and experiences that perfectly fit His will for us.[1]

If we are to be effective preachers and pastors, we must resolve to be godly. We must have a growing, varied, and unique life with God in order to mortify worldliness and avoid self-destruction. Baxter warned ministers, "You have heaven to win or lose for yourselves as much as others."[2] On the Great Day of Judgment, will we be standing with those who plead with Christ, "Lord, Lord, have we not prophesied in thy name?" (Matt. 7:22). If we have not truly walked with God, we will hear Christ say, "I never knew you: depart from me, ye that work iniquity" (v. 23).

16

YOUR FAMILY

orldliness often gives rise to selfishness, and selfishness profoundly affects important relationships. Too many of us ministers show how worldly we are by neglecting our wives and children. We are so busy with agendas, meetings, and the needs of people in our congregation that we are prone to forget the needs of those closest to us. We can *use* our wives more than we *serve* them, forgetting, as Abraham Booth says, that our wives are our "second selves."

Booth quotes a letter from a minister's wife in the nineteenth century that sounds as if it might have been written today:

> My husband is much esteemed among his religious acquaintance, as a respectable Christian character; but his example at home is far from being delightful. Little caring for my soul, or for the management of our growing offspring, he seems concerned for hardly any

131

thing more, than keeping fair with his people: relative to which, I have often calmly remonstrated, and submissively entreated, but all in vain. Surrounded with little ones, and attended with straits; destitute of the sympathies, the instructions, the consolations, which might have been expected from the affectionate heart of a pious husband, connected with the gifts of an evangelical minister, I pour out my soul to God, and mourn in secret.[1]

Take heed to your family.

The Relationship with Your Wife

The apostle Peter tells us, "Ye husbands, dwell with them [your wives] according to knowledge, giving honour unto the wife, as unto the weaker vessel, and as being heirs together of the grace of life; that your prayers be not hindered" (1 Peter 3:7). That implies several duties:

First, we must spend time with our wives. "Dwell with them," Peter says. The precious bond of oneness cannot be nurtured in our absence. Worldliness in ministers is often prone to increase because time and intimacy with our wives are not properly fostered.

Second, we must be considerate of our wives. They are made differently than we. "Dwell with them according to knowledge," Peter counsels—because they are weaker vessels. Notice he doesn't say "weak vessels," as if we are strong and they are weak. We men are weak, too; we all have our treasure in earthen vessels. But our wives are weaker than we are. Though they are certainly stronger in many ways, they are weaker physically and emotionally; that is, they need to be handled tenderly and with large dosages of love.

A minister should respect his wife's physical and emotional needs. He should have compassion for hormonal changes and struggles that he doesn't face. He ought to be a special model of Christian patience at such times.

Third, we must "honor" our wives, Peter says. We must respect them profoundly, nurture them consistently, and manifest fidelity toward them. We should never speak disparagingly about our wives as worldly men do. We ought to treat our wives as lovingly as Christ treats the church and speak about them as tenderly as Christ speaks about the church. Are we protecting, guiding, cherishing, loving, and complimenting our wives every day? Are we faithful leaders in the home? Is our marriage so godly that our entire congregation reads it as an epistle of grace?

Are we faithful to our wives in their presence and absence? Are we faithful to them in our actions, our speech, and our thoughts? Do we refuse to engage in any form of mental adultery or flirtation with other women? Do we keep our eyes and hearts from lusting after others? We should say as Job says, "I made a covenant with mine eyes; why then should I think upon a maid?" (Job 31:1). All this is involved in honoring our wives and overcoming a worldly attitude to marriage.

Finally, we must provide spiritual leadership for our wives. Since we are "heirs together of the grace of life," our prayer life must not be hindered. As husbands, we must pray every day alone with our wives, giving ourselves as couples to prayer (1 Cor. 7:5). We should never treat our wives badly, never run roughshod over their feelings, never be argumentative with them, for all such behavior hinders our prayer life with them.

If my wife and I are joint heirs of the grace of life, I must treat her like the queen and bride she is in the sight of the perfect Bridegroom, Jesus Christ. I must profoundly appreciate all the burdens she carries with me in the ministry, and not be the cause of additional burdens. I must love her as Christ loves the church (Eph. 5:25–27).

Christ loves the church *absolutely*. He gave *Himself* for His church (v. 25b). Do you give yourself, under God, first and foremost to your bride?

Christ loves the church *realistically*. He loves her despite her "spots" and "wrinkles" or "any such thing" (v. 27a). Do you love your wife despite her faults? Do you accept her as she is? Or do you perhaps put pressure on her as a minister's wife that promotes tension in your marriage and unrealistic expectations about her role in the congregation?

Christ loves the church *purposefully*. He loves her in order to "sanctify and cleanse [her] with the washing of water by the word," and so to present her "to himself a glorious church," that she "should be holy and without blemish" (vv. 26–27). Is your greatest desire for your wife that your attitude toward her as husband, your bringing of the Word to her, and your walk of life before her, might encourage her to walk in the King's highway of holiness and be always ready to meet her Lord at His appearing?

Christ loves the church *sacrificially*. He *gave* Himself for her (v. 25). Do you maintain a giving spirit toward your wife? Have you truly learned that also in marriage it is more blessed to give than to receive?

Do you love your wife in a sufficiently Christlike manner to lead her spiritually in the ways of God? God forbid that you show more spiritual care for your parishioners than for your wife!

The Relationship with Your Children

Priority must also be shown to our children in our teaching, training, and evangelizing. How are we managing our children? Are we, like the world, offering them possessions rather than time and attention? Are we training them in the ways of God, covenantally and evangelistically? Are we fulfilling our calling to be teaching prophets, interceding priests, and guiding kings to our own children? Do we engage in serious family worship and daily godly conversation with them, mentoring them in the truths we preach? Do we treat them according to their nature and needs, recognizing that each child is to be treated individually? Are we affectionate, supportive, and encouraging with each child?

The great theologian Charles Hodge ordered the doorknob of his study to be lowered sufficiently so that his smallest child would be able to have access to him at any time. Do our children know they have the privilege of a perpetual access into our lives and a place of priority in our hearts, just as we have in relation to our Father in heaven? Do we strive to treat them as our Father treats us?

Let us show the world the difference between a Christ-centered home and a worldly home. Let us show the world that a Christian wife will not chafe under the leadership of a husband who cherishes, protects, and guides her (Eph. 5:25–30). Let us show the world that children most often will respond in loving obedience when we manage our households aright, rearing them in the nurture and admonition of the Lord (Eph. 6:4; 1 Tim. 3:4–5).

135

YOUR FIGHT
AGAINST PRIDE

ake heed to your attitude toward ministry. Ministers can develop two paralyzing attitudes toward the ministry: pride or pessimism. Both are worldly at heart, for both show that the world is not crucified in us. In this chapter we will deal with pride, in the next two chapters with pessimism.

The Sin of Pride

God hates pride (Prov. 6:16–17). He hates the proud with His heart, curses them with His mouth, and punishes them with His hand (Ps. 119:21; Isa. 2:12; 23:9). Pride was God's first enemy. It was the first sin in Paradise and the last we will shed in death.

As a sin, pride is unique. Most sins turn us away from God, but pride is a direct attack upon God. It lifts our hearts above God and against God. Pride seeks to dethrone God and enthrone itself.

Pride also seeks to dethrone my neighbor. It always puts self-idolatry above neighbor-service. At root, pride breaks both tables of the law and all Ten Commandments.

Pride is complex. "It takes many forms and shapes and encompasses the heart like the layers of an onion—when you pull off one layer, there is another underneath," wrote Jonathan Edwards.

We ministers, who are always in the public eye, are particularly prone to the sin of pride. As Richard Greenham wrote, "The more godly a man is, and the more graces and blessings of God are upon him, the more need he hath to pray because Satan is busiest against him, and because he is readiest to be puffed up with a conceited holiness."

Pride feeds off nearly anything: a fair measure of ability and wisdom, a single compliment, a season of remarkable prosperity, a call to serve God in a position of prestige—even the honor of suffering for the truth. "It is hard starving this sin, whenas there is nothing almost but it can live upon," wrote Richard Mayo.[1]

If we think we are immune to the sin of pride, we should ask ourselves: How dependent are we on the praise of others? Are we more concerned about a reputation for godliness than about godliness itself? What do gifts and rewards from others say to us about our ministry? How do we respond to criticism from people in our congregation?

Our forefathers did not consider themselves immune to this sin. "I know I am proud; and yet I do not know the half of that pride," wrote Robert Murray M'Cheyne. Twenty years after his conversion, Jonathan Edwards groaned about the "bottomless, infinite depths of pride" left in his heart. And Luther said, "I am more afraid of pope 'self' than of the pope in Rome and all his cardinals."

Pride spoils our work. "It forms when pride has written the sermon, it goes with us to the pulpit," Richard Baxter said. "It forms our tone, it animates our delivery, it takes us off from that which may be displeasing to the people. It sets us in pursuit of vain applause from our hearers. It makes men seek themselves and their own glory."[2]

A godly minister fights against pride, whereas a worldly one feeds pride. "Men frequently admire me, and I am pleased," admitted Henry Martyn, but added, "but I abhor the pleasure I feel."[3] Cotton Mather recalled that when pride filled him with bitterness and confusion before the Lord, "I endeavoured to take a view of my pride as the very image of the Devil, contrary to the image and grace of Christ; as an offense against God, and grieving of His Spirit; as the most unreasonable folly and madness for one who had nothing singularly excellent and who had a nature so corrupt."[4] Thomas Shepard also fought pride. In his diary entry for November 10, 1642, Shepard wrote, "I kept a private fast for light to see the full glory of the Gospel . . . and for the conquest of all my remaining pride of heart."[5]

Can you identify with these pastors in your struggle against pride? Do you care enough about your brothers in ministry to admonish them about this sin? When John Eliot, the Puritan missionary, noticed that a colleague thought of himself too highly, he would say to him, "Study mortification, brother; study mortification."[6]

Ways to Subdue Pride

How do we fight against pride? Here are some ways to help you subdue pride:

• Understand how deeply rooted pride is in us, and how dangerous it is to our ministry. We should remonstrate with ourselves like the Puritan Richard Mayo: "Should that man be proud that has sinned as thou hast sinned, and lived as thou hast lived, and wasted so much time, and abused so much mercy, and omitted so many duties, and neglected so great means?—that hath so grieved the Spirit of God, so violated the law of God, so dishonoured the name of God? Should that man be proud, who hath such a heart as thou hast?"[7]

• Consider Christ. If we would kill worldly pride and live in godly humility, let us look at our Savior, whose life, Calvin said, "was naught but a series of sufferings." Nowhere was humility so cultivated as at Gethsemane and Calvary. When pride threatens you, consider the contrast between a proud minister and our humble Savior. Confess with Joseph Hall:

> Thy garden is the place,
> Where pride cannot intrude;
> For should it dare to enter there,
> 'Twould soon be drowned in blood.

And sing with Isaac Watts:

> When I survey the wondrous cross,
> On which the Prince of glory died;
> My richest gain I count but loss,
> And pour contempt on all my pride.

• Stay in the Word. Read, search, memorize, love, pray over, and meditate upon such passages as Psalm 39:4–6, Psalm 51:17, Galatians 6:14, Philippians 2:5–8, Hebrews 12:1–4, and 1 Peter 4:1, all in dependency upon the Spirit. The Spirit alone can break the back of our pride and cultivate humility within us by taking the things of Christ and showing them to us.

• Seek a deeper knowledge of God, His attributes, and His glory. Job and Isaiah teach us that nothing is so humbling as knowing God (Job 42; Isa. 6). Spend time meditating on God's greatness and holiness in comparison to your smallness and sinfulness.

• Practice humility (Phil. 2:3–4). Remember how Augustine answered the question "What three graces does a minister need most?" by saying, "Humility. Humility. Humility." To that end, seek greater awareness of your depravity and the heinousness and irrationality of sin. Don't rest until you can confess with John the Baptist on a daily basis, "He [Christ] must increase, but I must decrease" (John 3:30), for that is the essence of humility.

• Remember daily that "pride goeth before destruction, and a haughty spirit before a fall" (Prov. 16:18). View your afflictions as God's gifts to keep you humble. View your talents as gifts of God that never accrue any honor to you (1 Cor. 4:7). Everything you have or have ever accomplished has come from God's hand.

• View overcoming pride as a lifelong process that calls you to grow in servanthood. Be determined to fight the battle against pride by considering each day as an opportunity to forget yourself and serve others. As Abraham Booth writes, "Forget not, that the whole of your work is ministerial; not legislative—that you are not a lord in the church, but a servant."[8] The act of service is intrinsically humbling.

• Read the biographies of great saints, such as Whitefield's *Journals, The Life of David Brainerd,* and Spurgeon's *Early Years.* As Martin Lloyd-Jones says, "If that does not bring you to earth, then I pronounce that you are just a professional and beyond hope."[9] Associate, too, with living saints who exemplify humility, rather than arrogant or flattering people.

• Meditate much on what the Puritans called "the four last things": the solemnity of death, the certainty of Judgment Day, the vastness of eternity, and the fixed states of heaven and hell. Consider what you deserve on account of sin and what your future will be on account of grace; let the contrast humble you (1 Peter 5:5–7).

18

YOUR COPING WITH CRITICISM

A pessimistic attitude in a minister is no better than a proud one, for pride is usually the root of pessimism. Ministers become pessimistic when they think they deserve better treatment than they're getting. At times they may be right, but they may also be failing to exercise self-denial as their Master did, who suffered far worse at the hands of men than they will ever suffer, yet did not retaliate (1 Peter 2:23).

Resentment and criticism are the maidservants of pessimism. A complaining spirit produces negativism, depression, bitterness, and disillusionment in the ministry. It also promotes smugness and blindness to one's own condition. Bitter ministers often don't see their unforgiving spirit, their habit of backbiting, or their tendency to judge others and magnify their deficiencies (Matt. 7:3–5).

If any minister had reason to be pessimistic, it was the imprisoned Paul. Yet Paul wrote his most joyous epistle, Philippians, from prison. Paul knew times of inner gloom and depression (2 Cor. 1:8–9), but his epistles show little evidence of it. He could say, "For I have learned, in whatsoever state I am, therewith to be content" (Phil. 4:11). People have enough troubles and burdens without having to endure the ministrations of a pessimistic, discontented pastor.

Part of the problem of pessimism is that few ministers know how to respond to those who criticize them. They've received no advice in seminary on this critical matter, can find little helpful literature on it, and most likely, have heard no conference addresses about it. In a recent study, 81 percent of American clergymen said they have experienced hostile criticism. Twenty-five percent felt that coping with criticism was the most difficult problem of ministry.[1] Being on the receiving end of criticism for many years often results in pessimism, cynicism, exasperation, insomnia, and even resignations. This chapter provides some helps to cope with criticism without letting it lead to pessimism.

Consider Criticism Inevitable

John Wesley once questioned in his journal if he was truly right with God since he had received no criticism for the entire day! It is futile to think that you can avoid criticism in the ministry. Ministers engage in what Andy Stanley calls "visioneering." Implementing visions involves bringing about change, and change prompts criticism from those who are accustomed to the status quo.[2] Besides, if you proclaim the whole counsel of God as you should, you are bound to become a target of criticism, for the truths you bring are of eternal consequence. Don't be surprised, therefore, when people either hate you or love you. If you're getting through to them, few will feel neutral toward you. They'll either reject your message, or testify that it feeds their soul. As Jesus says in Luke 6:26, "Woe unto you, when all men shall speak well of you." So, expect criticism; don't be devastated by it.

Consider the Motive

It is imperative, first of all, to listen well. Don't only get the facts straight, but also ask: Have I heard and understood the criticism rightly and accurately? Have I heard the real problem or just a symptom of something deeper? Unresolved anger, depression, changes in life situations, frustration in relationships, jealousy, shattered expectations, and dissatisfaction with church work can lead to criticism. So ask yourself, "Does the person who is criticizing me have a proper motive which aims at the genuine improvement of my ministry, or is it indicative of something else? For example, does the critic enjoy finding fault because it somehow makes him feel superior?" Understanding the person's motive will help you respond and cope better with the criticism. As a general rule, give your critic the benefit of the doubt; assume that his motive is pure, unless you have convincing evidence otherwise.

Consider the Source

Though you should take every critic seriously, still ask yourself: Who is criticizing—an office-bearer, a mature believer, a babe in grace, an unbeliever, a highly critical individual, or a fringe member of the church? James Taylor writes, "Those who criticize are usually those on the fringe, who stand back and are deaf to every appeal for service."[3] Criticisms from such persons seldom merit change or any other investment of energy on your part.

On the other hand, if the critic is a mature believer or an office-bearer who is usually supportive, you should consider the criticism far more seriously and will often find some truth in it that calls for change. What's more, you should encourage constructive evaluation from such people. Generally speaking, the more you can sincerely welcome constructive criticism, the more your ministry and relationships with others will benefit from it.

Be careful, however, not to respond excessively to complaints that are raised by few and have little substance to them. There is, of course, a difference between an insubstantial complaint being raised by three people in a congregation of fifteen and by three people in a congregation of one thousand. In a large congregation, a change made for a few will often provoke more persons than the change satisfies. In short, the quality of the complaint must take priority, but sometimes the number of persons complaining also merits undertaking a change that is otherwise inconsequential.

Consider the Context

The physical setting, timing, and situation out of which criticism comes may help us determine whether the criticism is helpful. As a general rule, don't respond to criticism for at least twenty-four hours to allow yourself time for prayer, sifting through your feelings, getting past some of the hurt, and consulting others whose wisdom you respect.

Prayer-time is critical. Prayer puts criticism in its proper context. It provides clarity of mind and warmth of soul, decreases

145

your anxiety level, and rekindles your passion for what is right and true.

Remember, you are known more for your *reactions* than your *actions* (Prov. 16:32). Forcing solutions to issues too hastily may make a bad situation worse. Some situations will yield only to the healing touch of time. Truth has a way of eventually vindicating itself. Luke 21:19 says, "In your patience possess ye your souls."

Consider Yourself

Critics are often God's gifts to guard us from self-satisfied and self-destructive tendencies. The Holy Spirit uses our critics to keep us from justifying, protecting, and exalting ourselves. Although critics often exaggerate their case and are seldom entirely right, they are often partially right.

Ask yourself, "Am I responding appropriately to criticism?" Remember, those who have an ear for Christ learn to have an ear for others also. If you find yourself habitually feeling slighted, neglected, and mistreated, view your feelings with suspicion. Let yourself be more vulnerable. You will complain less if you consider how little criticism you receive, though you are unworthy, compared with Christ, who is perfectly worthy.

Find some accountability partners to monitor your reactions. Seek the wisdom and courage needed to penetrate the insulation around your ego. Don't be afraid to say, "I was wrong; will you forgive me?"

Consider the Content

You can learn valuable truths about yourself from critics. Be grateful for that. Some of our best friends are those who disagree with us lovingly, openly, and intelligently. "Faithful are the wounds of a friend" (Prov. 27:6). Helpful criticism is like good medicine.

David Powlison writes, "Critics, like governing authorities, are servants of God to you for good (Rom. 13:4). He who sees into hearts uses critics to help us see things in ourselves: outright failings of faith and practice, distorted emphases, blind spots, areas of neglect, attitudes and actions contradictory to stated commitments, and, yes, strengths and significant contributions."[4]

So ask yourself, What are the critics saying that might help me improve myself and my ministry? Is there a kernel of truth in this particular criticism that, if changes are made, will make me a better minister?

If critics say something constructive, absorb it, confess your fault, take the lead in self-criticism, ask for forgiveness wholeheartedly, make changes for the better, and move on. If they offer nothing constructive, be kind and polite, and move on.

Don't ever get self-defensive or angry, but turn the other cheek, as Jesus advised. If your conscience is clear, a simple, straightforward explanation may be helpful in certain cases, though respectful silence is often more appropriate and effective (Mark 14:61). At all costs, don't strive to justify yourself; your friends don't need that, and your enemies probably won't believe you anyhow. Refuse to descend to the level of the negative critic; don't render evil for evil. Fight God's battles, not your own, and you will discover that He will fight yours. It is not for you to repay. Romans 12:19 says, "Dearly beloved, avenge not yourselves, but rather give place unto wrath: for it is written, Vengeance is mine; I will repay, saith the Lord."

Don't take every whisper seriously. Don't get sidetracked into fruitless controversy, or spend your energy trying to appease or persuade implacable critics who foster animosity. Remember, "A brother offended is harder to be won than a strong city: and their contentions are like the bars of a castle"

(Prov. 18:19). But do ask: Why am I being misunderstood? Do my sermons, attitudes, "hobby horses," and personal traits somehow combine to send a mixed message? Am I only implying what I should make explicit, or am I ignoring certain problems that should be addressed? Often your critics will be at least partially right in one or more of these areas; at the very least, they will teach you patience, make you more like Christ, and keep you from pride. They can save you from yourself and lead you to greater dependency on God.

Whatever results the criticism yields, once you've dealt with it and implemented the necessary changes, do not let it fester inside of you. Develop the attitude of Eleanor Roosevelt, who said, "Criticism makes very little dent upon me, unless I think there is some real justification and something should be done." Either way, deal with the criticism quickly and efficiently, and put it behind you. Then bury yourself in your work. Remember, pessimism develops when we harbor the memory and hurt of criticism, allowing it to fester inside.

Consider Scripture

Some ministers are so delicate that they cannot endure criticism without crumbling. They need to develop better emotional muscle. Other ministers are so battle-hardened by the ministry that their hearts are, as someone said, like the hide of a rhinoceros. They need to develop the tender heart of a child. Actually, we need both; we need to cultivate the heart of a child for biblical criticism and the hide of a rhinoceros for satanic criticism. That combination is possible, not in our strength, but only through God's grace molding our hearts by His Word.

We need to memorize and meditate upon texts such as Ephesians 6:10, "Be strong in the Lord, and in the power of his might," as well as Romans 12:10, "Be kindly affectioned one to another with brotherly love," and Romans 8:28, "And we know that all things work together for good to them that love God, to them who are the called according to his purpose." Let us not forget that God makes no mistakes. Look more to Him as the ultimate cause rather than to secondary causes. Believe Jesus when He says in John 13:7, "What I do thou knowest not now; but thou shalt know hereafter." We ought to read and meditate upon such texts every day, and let them permeate our minds and souls, so that we are persuaded that the purposes of our Lord will always prevail, even in the heaviest of persecutions. Satan is not Christ's master; rather, Christ is master over Satan, and will use even satanic criticism for His own wise purposes. Accept, therefore, all Christ's providential dealings with you as from Himself, and let those dealings conform you to His image. Only as Scripture conforms us to the image of Christ will we find the right balance of strong tenderness and tender strength in the face of criticism.

Consider Christ

Above all, look to Jesus in the face of mounting criticism. Hebrews 12:3 advises, "Consider him that endured such contradiction of sinners against himself." Peter is more detailed: "Christ also suffered for us, leaving us an example, that ye should follow his steps: Who did no sin, neither was guile found in his mouth: Who, when he was reviled, reviled not again; when he suffered, he threatened not; but committed himself to him that judgeth righteously" (1 Peter 2:21–23). If Christ, who was perfect and altogether innocent, was spat upon, mocked, rejected, and crucified, what can we imperfect pastors expect? If one of Jesus' handpicked apostles betrayed Him for a paltry sum, and another swore that he did not know Him out of fear of a servant maid, why should we expect to carry on our ministries without ever being betrayed or deserted?

What's more, if our critics happen to be in error and we are suffering unjustly, shouldn't we thank God that they don't know how bad we truly are? No matter how much we are criticized, we are never criticized as much as our sin merits, even if we are innocent of the accusation levelled against us.

If we have Christ, who, being innocent, suffered infinitely more for our sake than we shall ever suffer for His sake, we have more than enough to cope with any trial (1 Cor. 10:13; 2 Cor. 4:7–12). Drink deeply of the love of Christ, find your delight in the Triune God, and you will conquer pessimism and be able to love your critic (Ps. 37:1–4).

Then, too, consider the faithfulness of Christ. Has He not been faithful to you in the past and brought you through every period of criticism? Is He not greater than any present obstacle? Rather than focusing on your critic who seems to wield so much power, focus on Christ's greater power and undying faithfulness as your Intercessor and Advocate at the Father's right hand (Heb. 7:25). Trust Him once more. He will not disappoint you.

Consider Biblical Saints

Allow me to present as illustrations one Old Testament and one New Testament saint. Consider Nehemiah. Many of Sanballat's criticisms were valid. Nehemiah's workers were not skilled; many were not committed. Some sections of the wall were not strong; some sections could not be rebuilt (Neh. 4:1–3). How did Nehemiah respond? He committed his cause to God in prayer. He remembered that the source of his vision was God and not himself. Then, by setting up a guard, he revised his plan according to circumstances without abandoning his vision (Neh. 4:4–9). This three-step response is often just what we need to do: pray, remember, revise—but don't abandon the vision! A failed plan does not equal a failed vision. Usually, it means that you must swallow your pride, then revamp or even redraft the plan so that the vision can be implemented better.[5]

Consider, too, the apostle Paul in 2 Corinthians. There he defends himself from the charges of the Corinthians who were challenging his leadership and criticizing him for not being a super-apostle, being physically weak, and having contemptible speech. How does Paul respond to these criticisms in chapter 10? He takes refuge in Christ. "We are Christ's," he says in verse 7. He shores up his identity in Christ's person and His work, according to the Scriptures and his own experience. Then he strives to take every thought captive to the obedience of Christ. Finally, he submits his every weakness into God's hands, accepts those weaknesses, and trusts that God will use him even as a broken clay pot to let the gospel light shine through him. Let us go and do likewise.[6]

Consider Love

Love the one who criticizes you. For Christ's sake, become better acquainted with those who criticize you; you cannot love those you don't know. Seek to understand them. Assure them that you want to learn from them and that you want iron to sharpen iron. Thank them for coming directly to you with their criticism.

Be willing to forgive any injury done to you. Failure to forgive will keep the pain alive. It will sour your preaching, cripple your ministry, and hinder your prayer life. As Spurgeon says, "Unless you have forgiven others, you read your own death warrant when you repeat the Lord's Prayer. Forgive and forget. When you bury a dead dog, don't leave its tail sticking up above the ground."

Pray *with* your critic. If he visits you, always begin with prayer, and ask him to close in prayer, unless he is still bitter at the end of the visit. (In the case of a woman or child, you should probably offer the closing prayer.) Be very careful to pray to God and not against your critic in your prayer. Go the extra mile to ask the Lord to forgive you and to help you change in any area that needs forgiveness and change. Be as specific as possible. Pray with integrity and humility.

And then pray *for* your critic in private. It's difficult to stay bitter against a person for whom you pray. The Lord delivered Job from his hard feelings toward his judgmental friends when he prayed for them. Praying for those who defame you produces peace of mind and freedom from most of the pain of criticism.

Feel pity for your negative critic. How unhappy such a person is! What damage habitually critical adults do to their children! How seldom do the children of critics become stalwart sons and daughters of the church! How tragic to be a parent who causes "these little ones to stumble"! Critical parents will have so much to answer for on the Judgment Day. Thank God that you are on the receiving end, not the criticizing end. That, too, is only by grace, for our natural hearts are no better or different.

Finally, put away anything that inhibits love. As Peter writes, "Laying aside all malice, and all guile, and hypocrisies, and envies, and all evil speakings" (1 Peter 2:1). Show kindness and attention. I feel so strongly about this that someone once said, "The best way to get attention from our minister is to become his enemy!"

There's another side benefit to this for you as well. You will discover that when you lovingly serve your critic rather than resentfully retaliate against him, your own wounds will heal more rapidly. If your critic rebuffs your attempt to serve him, reach out to serve others—comfort the needy, lift up the fallen, support the weak. That will be excellent therapy for you.

Consider Long-Term Vision

No president in American history was so respected and yet so reviled as Abraham Lincoln. Thousands opposed his views on war and slavery as well as his attempts to keep the nation united. One day a friend pulled Lincoln aside and told him that the criticism had reached such a crescendo that it was as if Lincoln were surrounded by scores of barking dogs. Lincoln responded, "You know that during the time of the full moon, dogs bark and bark at the moon as long as it is clearly visible in the sky." Puzzled by Lincoln's response, the friend asked, "What are you driving at? What's the rest of the story?" Lincoln answered, "There is nothing more to tell. The moon keeps right on shining."

You see, Lincoln believed that he was right and that his policies would in the long run win over critics and unify the country. As pastors, we can waffle too easily under the pressure of "barking parishioners" when we know we are in the right. To obtain temporary peace with a few disgruntled members, we are prone to abandon long-term biblical vision that shines on our churches and ministries like a full moon. Don't do that. Don't be intimidated by critics and criticism. Don't allow a few critics to force you into their molds, so that you live timid and hesitant lives, doing nothing, saying nothing, and worst of all, being nothing. Don't lose heart and don't give up.

Remember, the fear of criticism is usually a greater threat than criticism itself. Even as you feel the fear of man, let the fear of God propel you forward and upward. Retain long-term vision by fearing God more than man. In the long haul, as

Theodore Roosevelt said, "It is not the critic who counts, not the man who points out how the strong man stumbled, or where the doer of deeds could have done better. The credit belongs to the man who is actually in the arena; whose face is marred by the dust and sweat and blood; who strives valiantly; who errs and comes short again and again."

Consider Eternity

On the other side of Jordan, our faithful Savior will be waiting for us; He will never let us down. He loves us even though He knows everything about us, and He will take us to be with Him where He is forever. He will wipe away every tear from our eye and will prove to be the Friend who sticks closer than a brother. All wrongs will be made right. All injustices will be judged. All criticism will be past. All evil will be walled out of heaven and all good walled in.

Because of Jesus Christ, we will enjoy perfect fellowship and friendship with the Triune God, forever knowing, loving, and communing with the Father, the Son, and the Spirit. As a woman embracing her newborn forgets the pain of delivery, you will forget all the trials of your ministry when you embrace Immanuel.

In heaven there will be perfect unity. We will commune with the unfallen angels and the saints of all ages in absolute perfection. There will be no denominations, no divisions, no disagreements, no misunderstandings, no theological arguments, no ignorance. There will not be a hair's breadth of difference among the saints. Luther and Calvin will agree fully on every point. We shall all be one even as Christ is in the Father and the Father in Him. Our believing critics will embrace us, and we them. There will be a complete, perfect, visible, intimate oneness.

Three great truths shall become perfect reality for us: first, we will understand that all the criticism we received here below was used in the hands of our Potter to prepare us for Immanuel's land. Second, we will see fully that all the criticisms we were called to bear on earth were but a light affliction compared to the weight of glory that awaited us. Third, in heaven we will be more than repaid for every affliction we endured on earth for the sake of our best and perfect Friend, Jesus Christ.

Oh, happy day when this mortality shall put on immortality and this corruption, incorruption, and we shall ever be with the Lord! Let all the criticism our Sovereign God in His infinite wisdom calls us to endure in this life make us more homesick for the criticism-free land of Beulah where the Lamb is all the glory. There,

> The bride eyes not her garment
> But her dear Bridegroom's face.
> I will not gaze at glory,
> But on my King of grace;
> Not at the crown He gifteth,
> But on His pierced hand.
> The Lamb is all the glory
> Of Emmanuel's land.

Develop a Positive Attitude

Do we have a positive view of the ministry? We have the most important and significant vocation in the world. My father often said to me, "Your calling is more important than living in the White House!" We never have to wake up in the morning and ask if our ministry is a worthwhile pursuit. As Richard Baxter said, "I would not change my life for any of the greatest dignities on earth. I am contented to consume my body, to sacrifice to God's service, and to spend all that I have, and to be spent myself, for the souls of men."

We are ambassadors of the King of kings, and we have His promise that His Word shall not return to Him void (Isa. 55:10–11). Christ is our Intercessor at the right hand of the Father, and the Holy Spirit is the Advocate in our heart. God will not allow criticism beyond what He provides grace for us to bear (1 Cor. 10:13). Every criticism, like any other hardship or difficulty, will eventually work for our good (Rom. 8:28).

Stop your worldly complaining. Count your blessings. Persevere in the good fight of faith. You have the best of assurances in that fight—the promises of God; the best of advocates—the Holy Spirit; the best of generals—Jesus Christ; the best of results—everlasting glory. Follow Fred Malone's advice, "We must quit expecting people to respond properly, making them our tin gods of life and death. This is idolatry, to live and die upon our people's behavior. Paul said, 'Having received mercy, we faint not.' The comfort of God's mercy received is the only lasting motivation I have ever found to labor on in trial."[7]

"Lift up the hands which hang down, and the feeble knees; And make straight paths for your feet" (Heb. 12:12–13). For every look you take at yourself and your circumstances, look ten times at Christ, as Richard Baxter advised. You can start complaining when you have given as much for Christ as He has given for you. Gird up the loins of your mind, and stand fast, for your Savior is greater than both Apollyon and the times. Your Sender will not desert you. Hold fast your profession—even when friends desert you—by clinging to your High Priest who is holding fast to you. Trust Him. He's a Friend that sticks closer than a brother; He will never desert you. Don't put your trust in princes or in a dying, fallen world, but in the Prince of peace. Look Christward; lean Christward; pray Christward; preach Christward.

Put your hands again to the plow, despite your weakness and hurts. "Continue with double earnestness to serve your Lord when no visible result is before you," Spurgeon advised.[8] Pray more and look at circumstances less. "Bury not the church before she be dead," John Flavel quipped, and I would add: "Bury not yourself nor the church before you and she be dead." Believe Christ's promise to His servants in Isaiah 54:17, "No weapon that is formed against thee shall prosper; and every tongue that shall rise against thee in judgment thou shalt condemn. This is the heritage of the servants of the LORD, and their righteousness is of me, saith the LORD."

19

YOUR PREACHING

aking heed to ourselves is a great task. To that, the apostle adds, "and to all the flock" (Acts 20:28b). "As they that must give account" (Heb. 13:17), we are called to watch over those committed to our care. We are to be earnestly concerned for their knowledge of Christ and for their growth in grace. We are to diligently pray for them in private, preach to them from our pulpits, and counsel them in our homes.

Your Titles

In a helpful way, Scripture offers various titles that describe our roles so that we may wisely use our time and energy to tend to the needs of our flock. If we take these titles seriously, we will have no time or energy left to carry out our ministries in a flippant, worldly manner.

1. Be an *overseer* of the flock (Acts 20:28; 1 Peter 5:1–3), watching over and standing guard for the souls of all the flock, saved and unsaved. Feed and guide the church of God, which Christ has purchased with His blood; show them what it means to lead a holy life.

2. Be a *sower* of the Word (Ps. 126:5–6; Matt. 13:3). In dependence on the Spirit, work hard to prepare the soil of people's hearts, plant good seed in it, water and feed the tender plants of grace, and bring the harvest to maturity.

3. Be a *servant* of Christ among your people, and minister to them for His sake (2 Cor. 4:5). Do everything you can to advance the cause of God. Be faithful to each day's responsibilities. Take instructions from your Master and obediently follow them, becoming all things to all men within the boundaries of Scripture.

4. Be an *ambassador* for Christ. Our King sends us to negotiate treaties of peace between Him and those who are at enmity with Him. The words of 2 Corinthians 5:20 should burn in our souls: "Now then we are ambassadors for Christ, as though God did beseech you by us: we pray you in Christ's stead, be ye reconciled to God." Fulfill your commission by publishing overtures of peace and salvation (Isa. 55:1–7), insisting on the necessity of repentance as a prerequisite to forgiveness, on faith as the only way to Christ, and on holiness as the essential fruit of salvation. Preach with patience, remembering how slow you were to believe. Preach with urgency as "a dying man to dying men."

5. Be a *steward* of the house and mysteries of God (1 Cor. 4:1–2; Titus 1:7). You have been entrusted with the ministry of the Word and the sacraments. As a good steward of those means of grace, administer them with instructions, comforts, admonitions, warnings, and discipline to those entrusted to your care.

6. Be a *master builder* (1 Cor. 3:10) in the temple of God. Making Christ your foundation and chief cornerstone, work

with the gold, silver, and precious stones of true service to God rather than with the hay and stubble of works that will not endure the judgment fire.

7. Be a *watchman* (Ezek. 33:2–9) on the walls of Jerusalem. Do not cry peace to impenitent sinners; rather, sound the alarm to a guilty world. Labor to keep yourself pure from the blood of all men by faithful preaching, that you may save yourself and those who hear you. Remember that the world, Satan, and your own flesh are in league against you. Put on the whole armor of God, and trust God to give you strength. Endure hardness as a good soldier in God's army. Finish the work that the Lord Jesus has given you to do.

8. Above all, be a *preacher* of the Word (1 Tim. 2:7; 2 Tim. 4:2). "Feed the flock" means, first and foremost, *take heed to your preaching.*

Effective Preaching

Many ministers today compromise God's truth both in what they preach and in what they condone in worship. You don't need worldly humor or worldly illustrations to sustain your message. As Richard Baxter said, "You cannot break men's hearts by jesting with them. And Satan will not be charmed out of his possession. We must lay siege to the souls of sinners, and lay the battery of God's ordinance against them."[1]

Maintain the dignity of public worship and the pulpit. Your people don't come to church for entertainment; they come to hear the Word of God. Give it to them. You are to preach only the words of God. This is the sole reason why people listen to what we have to say. It is not because we have thought of something ingenious or profound to say. Nothing matters but what God has said. This is our solemn, simple task. As Martin Luther says, "When the preacher speaks, God speaks! And whoever cannot boast like that should leave preaching alone, for he surely denies and blasphemes God."

Work to penetrate the mind of God revealed in Holy Scripture. That is hard work, involving earnest prayer as well as the arduous task of exegesis: tracing the etymology of words, tracking down the intricacies of grammar, soaking oneself in the historical and cultural setting of the text, and laboring over points that express its meaning. Pray, study, meditate, and wrestle with God's words. Then seek with all your might to open up the mind of God to your flock with such simple clarity that even young children will understand you.

Remain a student of the Word of God. Search the Word, love the Word, embody the Word, and preach the Word. Let the Word of God master you, that you may master it. Let it mold you under the tutelage of the Spirit so you may mold your people through the true preaching of the Word.

When you are duly prepared, preach with authority. Preach biblically, doctrinally, practically, and experientially. Preach death in Adam and life in Christ. Aim to convict those who listen to you, knowing that the Holy Spirit will convict them through the preaching of God's Word. Labor to bring sinners to Christ. Aim to build up the children of God in the faith. Proclaim to the righteous in Christ that it shall be well with them; warn the unsaved, who are not in Christ, that they will be eternally punished unless they repent and believe the gospel.

Weak and foolish as it seems, preaching is what God uses to save sinners and to prepare His people for glory. Christ devoted Himself to preaching, in houses, synagogues, and the temple, and in the open air, on mountain tops, in the plains below, and even on the tossing blue waves of the Sea of Galilee. In so doing, He consecrated all the world as preaching ground. Paul and all the apostles were also called to preach, for Christ told them: "Go ye into all the world, and preach the gospel."

161

Preaching is our greatest work as ministers. It is important to visit the sick, to educate children, to lead consistory meetings, to counsel inquirers, even to write books, but the most important thing is to preach the Word. Preach the law to warn the unsaved and to direct the saved, preach the gospel to invite the unsaved to faith in the Lord Jesus Christ and to build up the saved in their faith. Let the pulpit be your watchtower, your throne, and your joy.

Focus your preaching on Christ. Beware of diversions, new techniques, catchy phrases, gimmicks, and games. Follow the example of Paul, who said to the Corinthians, "I determined not to know any thing among you, save Jesus Christ, and him crucified" (1 Cor. 2:2). This apostle who claimed to preach all the counsel of God also claimed to preach only Christ. That is to say, *to preach the whole counsel of God is to preach Christ.*

Paul does not say that Christ is only his primary focus; he says Christ is his *only subject.* Of course, Christ is the center of his message and its primary subject. But more than that, Paul says, "Christ is the sum and substance of what I preach." Apart from Christ crucified, there is nothing of equal value to talk about.

Today, we often divide up theology into categories: Christology, pneumatology, ecclesiology, soteriology, eschatology, and so on. This has its place for theological study, of course. But for Paul, Christology was the main heading under which every other subject fell. Everything we believe and have is in relation to Him. He is our only theme. Christ is the answer to every problem of worldliness. So, Paul would say, "He is all I preach. He is the sum and substance of my ministry. He is man's only hope, yes, but He is more. He is our highest incentive to holiness."

We have the words of eternal life, delivered to us by Christ Himself (John 6:68). The inherent value and significance of those words speak for themselves. They do not need the embellishment or art of our clever thoughts or contrivances.

We must preach Christ with love. Thomas Boston said, "We preach Christ so that you may fall in love with Him." Is that what our congregations hear from us? Do we preach with affection like Paul, who addressed the Galatians as "my little children, of whom I travail in birth again until Christ be formed in you" (Gal. 4:19)?

We must preach Christ with expectation. Do you have lost people in your congregation? If you want them converted, you must "preach to them as those who must be awakened here or in hell," Baxter said.[2] Do you want them to grow in grace? Then follow Thomas Brooks's advice: "Ministers must preach Christ feelingly, experimentally, as well as exemplarily. They must speak from the heart to the heart. They must feel the worth, the weight, and the sweet[ness] of those things upon their own souls that they would give out to others. It is only the preaching of Christ that changes the heart. This is what brings Christ and the soul together, and this is what keeps Christ and the soul together."[3]

In his first sermon at the Metropolitan Tabernacle, Spurgeon said, "I would propose that the subject of the ministry in this house, as long as this platform shall stand and this house be frequented with worshippers, shall be Jesus Christ in His person and His work." Fifteen years later, Spurgeon said to his theological students, "I have been preaching nothing but this name. That, brethren, is the magnet; He will draw His own to Himself. If we cry out to see conversion, this must be our preaching—more constant preaching of Christ. He must be in every sermon; He must be the top and bottom of all the theology that we preach."[4]

Take heed to preach Christ. That will save you and your flock from worldliness and promote godliness.

163

20

YOUR SHEPHERDING

All of the titles given in Scripture to ministers are within the parameters of Paul's exhortation to take heed to all the flock. But our clearest, broadest title is that of shepherd or pastor (Eph. 4:11). Paul mentions that specifically in Acts 20:28, "Feed [literally, 'be a shepherd to'] the church of God."

Sheep are unique creatures. They are among the most dependent, most foolish creatures on earth. They are prone to wander. They will leave rich pastures for barren ones, then not be able to find their way back. And they have stubborn wills, even to the point of battling those persons and those measures that would serve their best interests.

Without a shepherd's guidance, sheep will destroy themselves in one way or another. Without a shepherd, sheep cannot feed themselves, defend themselves against attack, or treat themselves when injured. Without their shepherd, sheep can do nothing.

Shepherding the church of God is an awesome task. Psalm 23 points out what we must cultivate as shepherds:

- A *heart* that beats with unconditional love for the flock of God
- A *hand* to guide God's sheep in paths of righteousness and to steer them away from sin
- An *eye* to keep our sheep from predators and to detect their backslidings
- An *ear* to hear their cries of distress
- *Knowledge* to recognize their diseases, joys, sorrows, strengths, and weaknesses
- *Skill* to lead them to pastures that meet their needs and to give them the right medicine for their ailments
- *Faithfulness* to stay with them in time of need
- *Strength* to use the rod of God's Word to beat them back to the right paths, and to use the staff to lift them up in difficulty, ever pointing them to the Good and Chief Shepherd, Jesus Christ[1]

Each of these shepherding qualities can be destroyed by a worldly spirit. How can you bind up the poor, wounded, and brokenhearted if your heart clings to worldly riches? How can you recover straying sheep if you're straying into the world yourself? How can you know the weaknesses, temptations, strengths, and gifts of the flock if you love the things of this world more than the people of God?

In *The Christian Ministry* Charles Bridges warns that a large proportion of our inefficiency as ministers may be traced to worldliness in us. Worldly ministers starve the sheep, rather than feed them. Among the dangers of worldliness are professionalism, petrification, a pleasure-focused ministry, frivolity, and indifference.

Worldliness Promotes Professionalism

Worldliness turns the ministry into a career, or mere job. Preaching, outreach, counseling, and visiting are no longer done under constraint of the divine call. Tasks are still done, but in a routine, dutiful way, void of a sense of the Spirit's call. Professional clerics too often feed on their professionalism. They love what Spurgeon called "ministerialism" more than ministry. They are pulpiteers rather than preachers, actors rather than appliers, self-centered rather than God-centered. They trust their own abilities rather than looking to Christ and His Spirit. In the end, their professionalism will destroy the sheep, for sheep need a personal, caring shepherd.

We must not think of our churches as work stations and our parishioners as cases; rather, we should think of our churches as hospitals where wounded people find loving, tender care. Like Jesus, we must suffer with our sheep. We can avoid the pitfall of professionalism only by loving the Lord of the church, His people, and the work He has called us to do. As Spurgeon said, "We shall never save more till we love more."[2]

Consider also what Horatius Bonar said about professionalism: "Love is wanting, deep love, love strong as death, love such as made Jeremiah weep in secret places for the pride of Israel. In preaching and visiting, in counseling and reproving, what formality, what coldness, how little tenderness and affection!"[3]

Worldliness Promotes Petrification

In the ministry, one either lives and grows or decays and petrifies. No matter how seasoned and experienced a pastor is, he must keep growing spiritually and intellectually. Worldliness stunts such growth. It keeps ministers from living on the growing edge.

The apostle Paul aimed to never stop growing. While he was in prison, waiting for the executioner's axe, Paul asked Timothy to bring his "books and parchments" (2 Tim. 4:13) so he could continue his studies.

One way to avoid petrification is to work at various levels. For example, teach and write below your level in some ministry to children. At the same time, preach, teach, and write at your present level. Then, too, stretch and grow by studying material above your level. Today we have unlimited opportunities for growth. We have rich personal libraries, the Internet, seminars, conferences, and countless other resources.

We cannot afford to waste our time or give way to laziness. We should pray much, meditate often, and study hard. We should read the best books and learn how to use them profitably. We should organize every hour of our time, yet remain flexible to respond to the needs of our people. We should remember three D's: *dump* the unnecessary paperwork, *delegate* whatever we can, and *deal* with every item only one time.

George Whitefield's diary says he was on his knees weeping over having wasted thirty minutes in a day. Every minister should be able to say with Napoleon, "I may lose battles, but no one will ever see me lose minutes, either by overconfidence or sloth." We note in passing that it is not wasting time to refresh our minds and bodies with seasonable rest and wholesome recreation. In the view of the Westminster divines, the sixth commandment requires us to make moderate and "sober use of meat, drink, physick, sleep, labour, and recreations" (*Larger Catechism*, Questions 135–36).

Nonetheless, with so many opportunities for ministry today, we have no excuse for idleness. Let us confess with Horatius Bonar: "Precious hours and days have been wasted in sloth, in

OVERCOMING THE WORLD IN THE MINISTRY

company, in pleasure, in idle or desultory reading, that might have been devoted to the closet, the study, or the pulpit. Indolence, self-indulgence, fickleness, flesh-pleasing, have eaten like a canker into our ministry, arresting the blessing and marring our success."[4]

Worldliness Promotes a Pleasure-Focused Ministry

When a minister speaks more about sports than about Christ, spends more time with a newspaper than with the Bible, more time cruising the Internet than in prayer, more time accumulating material possessions than promoting the welfare of the souls of his flock, his pleasure-seeking will undercut his ministry. At the end of the day, the man who focuses more on temporary pleasures than on godly disciplines may well succumb to alcoholism or adultery or some other sin of the flesh. In every case, the sheep are the losers. Can we expect the flock's level of holiness to rise above that of its earthly shepherd?

We need to shun every form of materialism. Our homes, cars, furniture, possessions, and clothing should not become ends in themselves. It is not right for a minister to walk "in a vain show" (Ps. 39:6). If we preach to our people that they may not set their hearts on earthly things while our lifestyle shows that we ourselves do, our ministry loses credibility.

Our daily conversation should not focus too much on earthly things, either. If we tell people that "out of the abundance of the heart, the mouth speaketh," and our conversation centers more on earthly possessions and pursuits than on our heavenly inheritance, our ministry loses credibility. Anything we do or say that puts earthly pleasure first and divine service last destroys the effectiveness of our ministry.

Materialism is dangerous because it is the practice of covetousness. Covetousness rules us from within. It is like a flood that bursts the banks of our hearts and spills over into our lives, wreaking destruction. Covetousness forgets that happiness does not consist in *things* but in *thoughts*. Don't let money, possessions, and fleshly desires become more important to you than usefulness to God and His people. Such covetousness will empty and diminish you. It will sour your taste for ministry.

God hates covetousness because it excludes and insults Him and callouses us. Brothers in the ministry, let us crucify covetousness and walk worthy of our calling. Don't think of ministry in terms of a salary but as a spiritual investment that offers eternal dividends. Like Paul, let us learn to be abased and to abound with contentment.

As Ralph Turnbull wrote, "The minister is a fool in this realm as in others, but let him know that he need not covet any man's possessions, not even his library or his church or his stipend or his popularity, for, with our limited opportunities and slender resources, we can, under God, be wealthy in the spirit of the sacrifice of the Cross."[5]

Covet no man's gifts. Use the talents God has given you. When Robert Murray M'Cheyne visited Israel, God used William Burns to usher in revival at M'Cheyne's church. M'Cheyne was as happy with the revival as if he had led the revival himself. He rejoiced in Burns's gifts. He followed God's more excellent way rather than the coveting ways of this world. "In lowliness of mind let each esteem other better than themselves" (Phil. 2:3).

Finally, don't covet women, and especially other men's wives. Walk circumspectly. Pray daily to be kept from temptation. Lean on the Spirit's strength. Thank Him for preserving you by removing desire when temptation was present and by removing temptation when desire was present.

Some practical advice: Don't visit a woman who is not at least twenty years older than you are without someone else in the home or office area. Refuse to engage in any form of flirtation. The best way to avoid coveting is to cultivate an excellent marriage with your wife and show your single-hearted devotion to her. Few women will attempt to flirt with you when they see how dedicated you are to your wife.

Think of these words of Isaiah: "Be ye clean, that bear the vessels of the LORD" (52:11). And remember this prayer of a pastor:

> I would be true, for there are those who trust me;
> I would be pure, for there are those who care;
> I would be strong, for there is much to suffer;
> I would be brave, for there is much to dare.

Remember, too, what Jesus said to His disciples, "Watch and pray, that ye enter not into temptation" (Matt. 26:41). It's as if Jesus said, "I have trained you. You have witnessed my example. But don't think that because you have been enrolled in the best seminary on earth you are beyond temptation. Watch and pray."

Watchfulness, prayer, and daily Bible-reading are the best antidotes for temptation. Few ministers have fallen who have maintained these spiritual disciplines. Take Abraham Booth's warning to heart: "Though I have had a greater share of esteem among religious people than I had any reason to expect; yet, after all, it is possible for me, in one single hour of temptation, to blast my character, to ruin my public usefulness, and to render my warmest Christian friends ashamed of owning me. Hold thou me up, O Lord, and I shall be safe!"[6]

Worldliness Promotes Frivolity

Ministers who lack sober-mindedness and convey no attitude of seriousness about life, the judgment to come, and eternity, create around themselves an atmosphere that quenches the fear of God. They instill in their people an attitude of complacency and indifference, leaving them asleep and unaware of the approach of danger.

There is a place for humor in the ministry, especially in private conversation. A minister is not supposed to be joyless, stuffy, and antisocial. But humor must be kept within bounds. And it must never degrade into something suggestive or indecent (Eph. 4:29; 5:12). Serious, godly conversation must be the heart of every visit we make. And every visit must be salted with prayer. Be like James Hervey who resolved "never to go into any company, where he could not obtain access for his Master."

Consider what Thomas Boston said: "When you are at any time in company, let something that smells of heaven drop from your lips. Learn that heavenly chemistry of extracting some spiritual thing out of earthly things. O what a shame it is for you to sit down in company, and rise again, and part with them, and never a word of Christ to be heard."[7]

If our conversation is not ruled by warm, caring sobriety, the spirit of worldly conversation will inevitably prevail. And worldly conversation is dominated, as Charles Bridge says, "by the fear of man, fleshly indulgence, and practical unbelief." There is no profit in multiplying words without knowledge (Job 35:16). We cannot edify those entrusted to our care if we engage them merely in worldly conversation. We will dishonor the Spirit by failing to speak of His work in the soul, and ought not be surprised when, in due course, any demand for godly conversation and godly living will be derided as legalism.

Worldliness Promotes Indifference

Like some doctors who see patients as numbers, some ministers treat people as objects to be manipulated rather than souls to be saved. Such ministers are wanting in prayer, lazy in sermon preparation, ineffective in preaching, and negligent in pastoral visitation.

Recently, I called on a woman in the hospital in response to the request of a relative. After visiting with her, I read Scripture with her, commented briefly on it, and closed with prayer. When I said goodbye, the woman wept and said, "My pastor came, too, but he talked more about himself and the weather than about my condition. He didn't read Scripture, didn't talk about the Lord, and his prayer was short and shallow. Do you think he cares about my soul?"

Brothers, if we're not going to pastor our people with both our minds and hearts, we should leave the ministry. An indifferent pastor is a hireling, not a shepherd. Horatius Bonar described such men well: "Associating too much and too intimately with the world, we have in a great measure become accustomed to its ways. Hence our tastes have been vitiated, our consciences blunted, and that sensitive tenderness of feeling which, while it turns not back from suffering yet shrinks from the remotest contact with sin, has worn off and given place to an amount of callousness of which we once, in fresher days, believed ourselves incapable."[8]

"God saves all kinds of people, even ministers," wrote John Kershaw, a nineteenth-century Baptist pastor. Though the ministry tends to isolate a pastor from the attractions of the world, one of the greatest dangers of ministry is that it allows a pastor to handle the sacred so frequently that it becomes banal to him. It is true that we can handle the Word of God as if it were no more than the words of men. We can take what is holy for granted as we live unholy lives. We can urge others to holiness but, like the Pharisees, not move an inch in that direction ourselves. Eventually, we operate our ministries more out of indifference and unbelief than faith.

Take heed, for indifference is the fruit of worldliness. It makes us cold in our preaching, slothful in our visiting, irreverent in handling eternal realities, and remiss in all our sacred duties.

Don't be overcome by a worldly, unbelieving spirit. Remember that everything that you say gets filtered through the grid of our people's minds. If the cumulative record of everything they know about you indicates more worldliness than godliness, our sheep will feel starved even while they feed on all our messages.

We cannot love both God and the world. We cannot serve two masters. How can we as ministers maintain our spiritual integrity, our love for God, our pastoral hearts, and our godly walk if we secretly flirt with the world? How can we live like a pilgrim and a sojourner when we long more for earth than heaven?

Take heed to the flock. Feed the church with the Word; do not starve them with worldliness. Heed the warning of Thomas Scott, "The minister who would not have his people give in to worldly conformity such as he disapproves, must keep at a considerable distance himself. If he walks near the brink, others will fall down the precipice."

21

YOUR PERSUASIONS
TO OVERCOME

The high calling of the ministry and the battle with worldliness can leave us feeling greatly defeated and discouraged. Happily, however, Paul supplies compelling persuasions to persevere and to overcome the world by faith.

Colaboring with the Sanctifying Spirit

"Take heed therefore unto yourselves, and to all the flock, over the which the Holy Ghost hath made you overseers," Paul counsels (Acts 20:28). We are serving as agents of the Holy Ghost, who has called us to our work, enables and equips us for it, and works both in us and in our people through the ministry of the Word. He has committed His sheep to our care.

That's why Paul says in 2 Corinthians 6:1 that we are "workers together with" the Spirit of God.

How can we comprehend that? We labor side by side with the Holy Spirit and not just with our fellow human office-bearers. We are agents of the Holy Ghost, fellow workers with God. It is our privilege to preach the gospel with the Holy Ghost sent down from heaven; the Word of God itself is the sword of the Spirit, and our ministry of the Word is the ministration of the Spirit (1 Peter 1:12; Eph. 6:17; 2 Cor. 3:8). Such an honor far outweighs the difficulties of church work. I often say to my wife, "I can handle a great deal of criticism when I see one sinner saved and one child of God growing under my ministry." Why? Because criticisms will fade, but God's work abides forever.

John Williams took more comfort from the conversion of one soul to God under his ministry than he did from seventy years of education, titles, and honors in church and state. Cotton Mather said, "The saving or enlightening or edifying, of one soul at any time, will be a matter of more joy unto you, than if all the wealth of Ophir should flow in upon you."[1] Samuel Rutherford said that meeting one of his parishioners from Anworth in heaven would make heaven to be two heavens for him.

There is nothing so humbling in all the world as being used by God to save souls from the abyss of hell and bring them to Jesus Christ and everlasting bliss. The greatest work on earth is to reveal the will of God to the church and to the world.

Cotton Mather wrote, "Of the ministry, it is the highest dignity, if not the greatest happiness, that human nature is capable of here in this vale below. To have the soul so far enlightened as to become the mirror, or conduit, or conveyor of God's truth to others, is our privilege." Thomas Scott said, "Had I a thousand lives, I would willingly spend them in [the ministry]: and had I as many sons, I should gladly devote them to it."[2] Edward Payson said there were times in his life when he clapped his hands in unrestrained joy that God had counted him worthy to be put into the ministry as His coworker.

If I am the Spirit's agent, I can say as did Nehemiah to those who opposed him, "I am doing a great work, so that I cannot come down: why should the work cease, whilst I leave it, and come down to you?" (Neh. 6:3). Our work is too important to let the world distract us from it, or allow worldliness to undercut it.

If, quite properly, we have a due sense of our own inadequacy and insufficiency to be the Spirit's coworkers, we may nonetheless be sure that we have a sufficiency from God (2 Cor. 3:5); that is, we have the help of the Spirit, enabling us to live in a godly manner, to put to death what is earthly in us, and to set our affection on things above; and so fight against worldliness in ourselves.

Purchase of the Sheep by the Redeeming Christ

Though the dignity of our work and its high privilege make us often cry with Paul, "Who is sufficient for these things?" we also confess with the apostle, "Therefore seeing we have this ministry, as we have received mercy, we faint not" (2 Cor. 4:1). We don't faint because the Spirit's persevering ministry in us is grounded in the atoning blood of Christ. Paul concludes with that glorious fact in Acts 20:28, "Take heed therefore unto yourselves, and to all the flock, over the which the Holy Ghost hath made you overseers, to feed the church of God, *which he hath purchased with his own blood.*"

We shepherd the church because Christ purchased the church of God with His blood. Our labor is difficult, but we do not faint because we do not do it for ourselves; we do it for Christ. Flavel reports Luther saying, "The labors of the ministry will exhaust the very marrow from your bones, hasten old age and death." But Flavel goes on to say, "Welcome pained breast, aching backs, and trembling legs if we can but approve ourselves Christ's faithful servants and hear that joyful voice from His mouth saying, 'Well done, good and faithful servant.' "

This moves us forward in the midst of difficulty: Christ has purchased the church with His own blood. He has bought her; she is His bride. When you grow weary, and your heart grows cold and indifferent, take heed of Christ, who says to you, "I died for them; will you not look after them? They were worth My blood; are they not worth your time, your tears, your prayers, your energy?"

Think about that when you become bone-weary in ministering to God's people. Say to yourself, "Christ has committed them to me at the price of His blood. These labors are worth every minute." Take heart, brothers; be humble, be hopeful. Labor with all your might for the sake and glory of Christ and His bride. Love Christ's sheep because He loved them, and washed them from their sins in His own blood (Rev. 1:5).

How can we persist in worldliness in the face of such a Savior? We must pursue our calling as ministers gripped by the conviction that we shall one day have to give account to the Chief Shepherd who laid down His life for the sheep. Being one of those sheep ourselves, we must daily bring all our personal and office-bearing sins to our Savior, anticipating the day when our mortality shall put on immortality and we shall serve Him in glory without blemish (1 Cor. 15). Kenneth MacRae, minister of the Free Church of Scotland, uttered these words five months before his death in 1964: "I have been long in His service here, but I never tired of it. All my grief was that it was so poor, so listless, so forgetful, and so lacking in holiness. But soon I shall serve Him with a perfect service, without failure and without fault."

Glorifying of the Electing Father

Finally, be persuaded to overcome worldliness by considering that God shall receive the glory from His church, including every faithful ministry. We are caring for the church of God—chosen by the Father from before the foundation of the world, loved with an everlasting love, and predestined to eternal life. We must reflect this electing love of God in our own love for the people to whom we minister. Love for the world is diametrically opposed to love for both God and His church (1 John 2:15).

All this is implied in our text, for we are called to "take heed" in response to "all the counsel of God" being declared (Acts 20:27). Our work, the Spirit's work, and the Son's work will help establish a redeemed church as the fruit of the Father's everlasting love to sinners and determination to glorify His own name. Sinners will be saved by the blood of His Son, the Spirit will empower the saved to grow in the grace and knowledge of the Lord Jesus Christ, and God will be glorified. That threefold, trinitarian purpose for our ministries should be enough to persuade us to abandon worldliness and to persevere in faithful ministry.

After all, it's the Triune God's glory, not ours, that's important. When Spurgeon had to leave England after a number of people were killed in Surrey Gardens, he was very discouraged. Even the sight of the Bible made him weep. But God comforted him with Acts 5:31, "Him hath God exalted with his right hand to be a Prince and a Savior," showing him that that was all that mattered. Spurgeon's response was, "If God is exalted, never mind what becomes of us. We are a set of pigmies; it is all right if *He* is exalted. God's truth is safe, we are perfectly willing to be forgotten, derided, slandered, or anything else that men please. The cause is safe, and the King is on the throne, Hallelujah! Blessed be His Name!"

Brothers, let us be lifted above discouragement. Our ministries serve the Triune God; what more could we ask for? For the Triune God's sake, "Take heed therefore unto yourselves, and to all the flock, over the which the Holy Ghost hath made you overseers, to feed the church of God, which he hath purchased with his own blood" (Acts 20:28).

If you have already given way to worldliness and feel too sinful to go on, consider John Robertson of Glasgow, who became so disillusioned with ministry that he decided to resign. One morning he prayed, "O God, Thou didst commission me forty years ago, but I have blundered and failed and I want to resign this morning." God showed Robertson that though he had blundered and failed, God was willing to forgive him. He saw that God wanted him to "re-sign," not resign, his commission.

That's God's will for you, too. Don't resign; *re-sign*. You do that the same way the backsliding Ephesians had to "re-sign" when they left their first love.

- *Remember,* therefore, from whence thou art fallen,
- *Repent* of your worldliness and backsliding,
- *Return* to your first love, ministry, and do the first works. (Rev. 2:5)

Don't give up on the Lord. He is not done with you or your ministry. Serve this great God with faithfulness and zeal. The world may not be worthy of you, but God is. Serve your Master with all your heart and every gift that you have. F. B. Meyer once said, "I have no special gifts. I am no orator, no scholar, no profound thinker. If I have done anything for Christ and my generation, it is because I have given myself to Jesus Christ, and then have tried to do whatever he wanted me to do."

179

Follow Spurgeon's advice: *"Be diligent in action."* Watch
for opportunities and be quick to seize upon them. Feed your
flocks as pastors, and increase them by being evangelists. Be
fruitful, and multiply, and replenish the earth. "We must use
every energy that we may checkmate the incessant activities of
the prince of darkness," Spurgeon declares.[3]

Finally, brothers, remember that your eternal day of rest will
soon dawn. On that day, Christ will raise you to Himself, saying, "Well done, thou good and faithful servant, enter now
into the joy of the Lord." He will wipe every tear from your
eye and embrace you as you enter glory. All shall be well. As
a woman seeing her newborn puts out of mind the pain of
delivery, you will forget all the trials of your ministry when
you embrace Immanuel. Then you will say with Peter, "Rejoice,
inasmuch as ye are partakers of Christ's suffering; that, when
his glory shall be revealed, ye may be glad also with exceeding
joy" (1 Peter 4:13). Soli Deo Gloria!

NOTES

Chapter 1: What Is Overcoming Worldliness?

1. Paul Brand and Philip Yancey, *In His Image* (Grand Rapids: Zondervan, 1984), 226–75.

2. Martin Lloyd-Jones, *Life in Christ: Studies in 1 John* (Wheaton, Ill.: Crossway, 2002), 215–16; cf. Joel R. Beeke, *Let's Study the Epistles of John* (Edinburgh: Banner of Truth Trust, 2005).

3. *The Psalter* (Grand Rapids: Reformation Heritage Books, 1999), 379.

4. C. H. Spurgeon, *The Metropolitan Pulpit* (Pasadena, Texas: Pilgrim Publications, 1977), 47:593.

5. Ibid., 594–95.

Chapter 2: Practicing the Overcoming Life

1. John R. W. Stott, *The Epistles of John: An Introduction and Commentary*, in *The New Testament Tyndale Commentaries* (Grand Rapids: Eerdmans, 1981), 174.

2. Joshua Harris, *Not Even a Hint* (Sisters, Ore.: Multnomah, 2003), 113–27.

3. John Blanchard, comp., *More Gathered Gold* (Hertfordshire, England: Evangelical Press, 1986), 249.

4. *Matthew Henry's Commentary* (McLean, Va.: MacDonald, 1985), 5:221 (on Matt. 15:28).

5. Cf. William Gurnall, *The Christian in Complete Armour* (Edinburgh: Banner of Truth Trust, 2002), 2:1–123.

6. Blanchard, *More Gathered Gold*, 341.

7. John Blanchard, comp., *Gathered Gold* (Hertfordshire, England: Evangelical Press, 1984), 339.

8. Ibid., 337.

Chapter 3: Making the Overcoming Last

1. Joel R. Beeke and Randall Pedersen, "Philip Henry," in *Meet the Puritans in Print* (Edinburgh: Banner of Truth Trust, 2005).

2. John Blanchard, comp., *Gathered Gold* (Hertfordshire, England: Evangelical Press, 1984), 337–38.

Chapter 4: What Is Piety?

1. Serene Jones, *Calvin and the Rhetoric of Piety* (Louisville: Westminster/John Knox Press, 1995). Unfortunately, Jones exaggerates Calvin's use of rhetoric in the service of piety.

2. Cited in I. John Hesselink, "The Development and Purpose of Calvin's Institutes," in *Articles on Calvin and Calvinism,* vol. 4, *Influences upon Calvin and Discussion of the 1559 Institutes,* ed. Richard C. Gamble (New York: Garland, 1992), 215–16.

3. See Brian A. Gerrish, "Theology within the Limits of Piety Alone: Schleiermacher and Calvin's Doctrine of God" (1981), reprinted in *The Old Protestantism and the New* (Chicago: University of Chicago Press, 1982), ch. 12.

4. John Calvin, *Institutes of the Christian Religion* [hereafter, *Inst.*], ed. John T. McNeill and trans. Ford Lewis Battles (Philadelphia: Westminster Press, 1960), 1:9.

5. See Lucien Joseph Richard, *The Spirituality of John Calvin* (Atlanta: John Knox Press, 1974), 100–101; Sou-Young Lee, "Calvin's Understanding of *Pietas,*" in *Calvinus Sincerioris Religionis Vindex,* ed. W. H. Neuser and B. G. Armstrong (Kirksville, Mo.: Sixteenth Century Studies, 1997), 226–33; H. W. Simpson, "*Pietas* in the *Institutes* of Calvin," in *Reformational Tradition: A Rich Heritage and Lasting Vocation* (Potchefstroom, South Africa: Potchefstroom University for Christian Higher Education, 1984), 179–91.

6. *John Calvin: Catechism 1538,* ed. and trans. Ford Lewis Battles (Pittsburgh: Pittsburgh Theological Seminary, 1972), 2.

7. *Inst.,* book 1, chapter 2, section 1. Hereafter the format 1.2.1 will be used.

8. *Inst.* 3.19.2.

9. *Institutes of the Christian Religion: 1536 Edition,* trans. Ford Lewis Battles, rev. ed. (Grand Rapids: Eerdmans, 1986). The original Latin title

reads: *Christianae religionis institutio totam fere pietatis summam et quidquid est in doctrina salutis cognitu necessarium complectens, omnibus pietatis studiosis lectu dignissimum opus ac recens editum (Joannis Calvini opera selecta,* ed. Peter Barth, Wilhelm Niesel, and Dora Scheuner, 5 vols. [Munich: Chr. Kaiser, 1926–52], 1:19 [hereafter, *OS*]. From 1539 on the title was simply *Institutio Christianae Religionis,* but the "zeal for piety" continued to be a great goal of Calvin's work. See Richard A. Muller, *The Unaccommodated Calvin: Studies in the Foundation of a Theological Tradition* (New York: Oxford University Press, 2000), 106–7.

10. *Calvin's New Testament Commentaries,* ed. David W. Torrance and Thomas F. Torrance, 12 vols. (Grand Rapids: Eerdmans, 1959–1972), *The Second Epistle of Paul the Apostle to the Corinthians, and the Epistles to Timothy, Titus and Philemon,* trans. Thomas A. Smail (Grand Rapids: Eerdmans, 1964), 243–44. Hereafter, *Commentary* [on text].

11. For the roots of Calvin's piety, see William J. Bouwsma, "The Spirituality of John Calvin," in *Christian Spirituality: High Middle Ages and Reformation,* ed. Jill Raitt (New York: Crossroad, 1987), 318–33.

12. *Inst.* 3.2.1; Calvin, *Ioannis Calvini opera quae supersunt omnia,* ed. Wilhelm Baum, Edward Cunitz, and Edward Reuss, *Corpus Reformatorum,* vols. 29–87 (Brunswick: C. A. Schwetschke and Son, 1863–1900), 43:428; 47:316. Hereafter, *CO.*

13. CO 26:693.

14. OS 1:363–64.

15. CO 24:362.

16. *Inst.* 3.7.1.

17. CO 26:225; 29:5; 51:147.

18. CO 49:51.

19. CO 26:166; 33:186; 47:377–78; 49:245; 51:21.

20. CO 6:9–10.

21. CO 26:439–40.

Chapter 5: Communion with Christ

1. "The *Unio Mystica* and the Assurance of Faith according to Calvin," in *Calvin: Erbe und Auftrag: Festschrift für Wilhelm Heinrich Neuser zum 65. Geburtstag,* ed. Willem van 't Spijker (Kampen: Kok, 1991), 78.

2. See e.g., Charles Partee, "Calvin's Central Dogma Again," *Sixteenth Century Journal* 18.2 (1987): 194; Otto Gründler, "John Calvin: Ingrafting in Christ," in *The Spirituality of Western Christendom,* ed. Rozanne Elder (Kalamazoo, Mich.: Cistercian, 1976), 172–87; Brian G. Armstrong, "The Nature and Structure of Calvin's Thought according to the *Institutes:*

Another Look," in *John Calvin's Magnum Opus* (Potchefstroom, South Africa: Institute for Reformational Studies, 1986), 55–82; Guenther Haas, *The Concept of Equity in Calvin's Ethics* (Waterloo, Ont.: Wilfrid Laurier University Press, 1997).

3. *Inst.* 3.11.9. See also CO 15:722.

4. Howard G. Hageman, "Reformed Spirituality," in *Protestant Spiritual Traditions,* ed. Frank C. Senn (New York: Paulist Press, 1986), 61.

5. *Inst.* 3.2.24.

6. Dennis Tamburello points out that "at least seven instances occur in the *Institutes* where Calvin uses the word *arcanus* or *incomprehensibilis* to describe union with Christ" (2.12.7; 3.11.5; 4.17.1, 9, 31, 33; 4.19.35; *Union with Christ: John Calvin and the Mysticism of St. Bernard* [Louisville: Westminster/John Knox Press, 1994], 89, 144). See also William Borden Evans, "Imputation and Impartation: The Problem of Union with Christ in Nineteenth-Century American Reformed Theology," Ph.D. diss., Vanderbilt University, 1996, 6–68.

7. *Commentary* on John 6:51.

8. *Inst.* 2.16.16.

9. Willem van 't Spijker, "*Extra nos* and *in nos* by Calvin in a Pneumatological Light," in *Calvin and the Holy Spirit,* ed. Peter DeKlerk (Grand Rapids: Calvin Studies Society, 1989), 39–62; Merwyn S. Johnson, "Calvin's Ethical Legacy," in *The Legacy of John Calvin,* ed. David Foxgrover (Grand Rapids: Calvin Studies Society, 2000), 63–83.

10. OS 1:435–36; Willem van 't Spijker, "*Extra nos* and *in nos* by Calvin in a Pneumatological Light," 44.

11. *Inst.* 3.1.4.

12. *Inst.* 4.17.6; *Commentary* on Acts 15:9.

13. *Commentary* on Ephesians 5:32.

14. *Inst.* 3.1.1; 4.17.12.

15. "Calvinus Vermilio" (#2266, 8 Aug 1555), CO 15:723–24.

16. CO 50:199. See also Barbara Pitkin, *What Pure Eyes Could See: Calvin's Doctrine of Faith in Its Exegetical Context* (New York: Oxford University Press, 1999).

17. *Inst.* 2.9.2; *Commentary* on 1 Peter 1:25. See also David Foxgrover, "John Calvin's Understanding of Conscience," Ph.D. diss., Claremont, 1978, 407ff.

18. *The Commentaries of John Calvin on the Old Testament,* 30 vols. (Edinburgh: Calvin Translation Society, 1843–1848), on Genesis 15:6. Hereafter, *Commentary* on text. See also *Commentary* on Luke 2:21.

19. *Inst.* 3.2.6.

20. *Inst.* 3.2.30–32.

21. *Inst.* 3.2.24; *Commentary* on 1 John 2:12.

22. *Sermons on the Epistle to the Ephesians,* trans. Arthur Golding (1577; reprint, Edinburgh: Banner of Truth Trust, 1973), 1:17–18. Hereafter, *Sermon* on Ephesians text.

23. *Commentary* on Ephesians 3:12.

24. *Sermon* on Ephesians 3:14–19.

25. *Commentary* on Habakkuk 2:4.

26. "The Third Part of Christian Freedom Misplaced," in *Later Calvinism: International Perspectives,* ed. W. Fred Graham (Kirksville, Mo.: Sixteenth Century Journal, 1994), 484–85.

27. *Inst.* 3.11.1.

28. *Sermons on Galatians,* trans. Kathy Childress (Edinburgh: Banner of Truth Trust, 1997), 2:17–18. Hereafter, *Sermon* on Galatians text.

29. *Inst.* 3.11.2.

30. Ibid.

31. *Inst.* 3.11.1; 3.15.7.

32. *Inst.* 3.13.1.

33. *Inst.* 1.7.5.

34. *Commentary* on John 17:17–19.

35. *Inst.* 3.11.6.

36. *Sermon* on Galatians 2:17–18.

37. *Commentary* on Romans 6:2.

Chapter 6: Piety and the Church

1. *Inst.* 4.1.1, 3–4; See also Joel R. Beeke, "Glorious Things of Thee Are Spoken: The Doctrine of the Church," in *Onward, Christian Soldiers: Protestants Affirm the Church,* ed. Don Kistler (Morgan, Pa.: Soli Deo Gloria, 1999), 23–25.

2. *Inst.* 4.1.4–5.

3. *Commentary* on Psalm 20:10.

4. *Commentary* on Romans 12:6.

5. *Commentary* on 1 Corinthians 12:12.

6. *Commentary* on 1 Corinthians 4:7.

7. *Commentary* on Ephesians 4:12.

8. *Commentary* on Psalm 18:31; 1 Corinthians 13:12; *Inst.* 4.1.5, 4.3.2.

9. *Sermons of M. John Calvin, on the Epistles of S. Paule to Timothie and Titus,* trans. L.T. (1579; reprint facsimile, Edinburgh: Banner of Truth Trust, 1983), 1 Timothy 1:8–11. Hereafter, *Sermon* on text.

10. *Calvin: Theological Treatises,* ed. J. K. S. Reid (Philadelphia: Westminster Press, 1954), 173. See also Brian Armstrong, "The Role of the Holy Spirit in Calvin's Teaching on the Ministry," in *Calvin and the Holy Spirit,* ed. P. DeKlerk (Grand Rapids: Calvin Studies Society, 1989), 99–111.

11. *Selected Works of John Calvin: Tracts and Letters,* ed. Henry Beveridge and Jules Bonnet (1849; reprint, Grand Rapids: Baker, 1983), 2:56, 69.

12. *Institutes of the Christian Religion: 1536 Edition,* 36.

13. *Inst.* 2.7.12. Calvin gleans considerable support for his third use of the law from the Davidic psalms (See also *Inst.* 2.7.12 and his *Commentary on the Book of Psalms,* trans. James Anderson, 5 vols. [Grand Rapids: Eerdmans, 1949]).

14. I. John Hesselink, "Law—Third Use of the Law," in *Encyclopedia of the Reformed Faith,* ed. Donald K. McKim (Louisville: Westminster/John Knox, 1992), 215–16. See also Edward A. Dowey Jr., "Law in Luther and Calvin," *Theology Today* 41.2 (1984): 146–53; I. John Hesselink, *Calvin's Concept of the Law* (Allison Park, Pa.: Pickwick, 1992), 251–62.

15. Joel Beeke and Ray Lanning, "Glad Obedience: The Third Use of the Law," in *Trust and Obey: Obedience and the Christian,* ed. Don Kistler (Morgan, Pa.: Soli Deo Gloria, 1996), 154–200; W. Robert Godfrey, "Law and Gospel," in *New Dictionary of Theology,* ed. Sinclair B. Ferguson, David F. Wright, J. I. Packer (Downers Grove, Ill.: InterVarsity Press, 1988), 379.

16. *Inst.* 4.14.1.

17. *Inst.* 4.16.9; Ronald S. Wallace, *Calvin's Doctrine of the Word and Sacrament* (London: Oliver and Boyd, 1953), 175–83. See also H. O. Old, *The Shaping of the Reformed Baptismal Rite in the Sixteenth Century* (Grand Rapids: Eerdmans, 1992).

18. *Inst.* 4.17.8–12.

19. Ibid.

20. *Inst.* 4.17.24, 33.

21. *Inst.* 4.17.12.

22. CO 9:47, 522.

23. *Inst.* 4.14.18.

24. *Commentary* on 1 Corinthians 11:25.

25. *Commentary* on Matthew 3:11; Acts 2:38; 1 Peter 3:21.

26. OS 1:136, 145.

27. *Inst.* 4.18.3.

28. *Inst.* 4.18.17.

29. *Inst.* 4.17.44.

30. *Inst.* 4.18.13.

31. "Calvin's Eucharistic Piety," in *The Legacy of John Calvin,* ed. David Foxgrover (Grand Rapids: CRC, 2000), 53.

32. *OS* 1:76.

33. Brian A. Gerrish, *Grace and Gratitude: The Eucharistic Theology of John Calvin* (Minneapolis: Fortress Press, 1993), 19–20.

34. Lionel Greve, "Freedom and Discipline in the Theology of John Calvin, William Perkins and John Wesley: An Examination of the Origin and Nature of Pietism," Ph.D. diss., Hartford Seminary Foundation, 1975, 124–25.

35. *CO* 31:19; translation taken from Barbara Pitkin, "Imitation of David: David as a Paradigm for Faith in Calvin's Exegesis of the Psalms," *Sixteenth Century Journal* 24.4 (1993): 847.

36. James Denney, *The Letters of Principal James Denney to His Family and Friends* (London: Hodder & Stoughton, n.d.), 9.

37. See James Luther Mays, "Calvin's Commentary on the Psalms: The Preface as Introduction," in *John Calvin and the Church: A Prism of Reform* (Louisville: Westminster/John Knox Press, 1990), 201–4.

38. Allan M. Harman, "The Psalms and Reformed Spirituality," *Reformed Theological Review* 53.2 (1994): 58.

39. *Commentary* on the Psalms, 1:xxxvi–xxxix.

40. Ibid., Psalm 5:11; 118:5.

41. Ibid., 1:xxxix. See James A. De Jong, " 'An Anatomy of All Parts of the Soul': Insights into Calvin's Spirituality from His Psalms Commentary," in *Calvinus Sacrae Scripturae Professor* (Grand Rapids: Eerdmans, 1994), 1–14.

42. *Commentary* on the Psalms, 1:xxxix.

43. John Walchenbach, "The Influence of David and the Psalms on the Life and Thought of John Calvin," Th.M. thesis, Pittsburgh Theological Seminary, 1969.

44. More than 30,000 copies of the first complete, 500-page Genevan Psalter were printed by over fifty different French and Swiss publishers in the first year, and at least 27,400 copies were published in Geneva in the first few months (Jeffrey T. VanderWilt, "John Calvin's Theology of Liturgical Song," *Christian Scholar's Review* 25 [1996]: 67). See also *Le Psautier de Genève, 1562–1685: Images, commentées et essai de bibliographie,* introduction by J. D. Candaus (Geneva: Bibliothèque publique et universitaire, 1986), 1:16–18; John Witvliet, "The Spirituality of the Psalter: Metrical Psalms in Liturgy and Life in Calvin's Geneva," in *Calvin Studies Society Papers, 1995–1997,* ed. David Foxgrover (Grand Rapids: CRC, 1998), 93–117.

45. Unlike Luther, Calvin tried to avoid mixing secular tunes with sacred singing and believed that all psalm-singing must be in the vernacular. The grounds for liturgical psalm-singing are found in the evidence of Scripture and in the practices of the ancient church (VanderWilt, "John Calvin's Theology of Liturgical Song," 72, 74).

46. Preface to the Genevan Psalter (1562); see Charles Garside Jr., *The Origins of Calvin's Theology of Music: 1536–1543* (Philadelphia: The American Philosophical Society, 1979), 32–33.

47. See *John Calvin: Writings on Pastoral Piety,* ed. and trans. Elsie McKee (New York: Paulist Press, 2001), part 3.

48. CO 10:12; cited in Garside, *The Origins of Calvin's Theology of Music,* 10.

49. Witvliet, "The Spirituality of the Psalter," 117.

50. W. Stanford Reid, "The Battle Hymns of the Lord: Calvinist Psalmody of the Sixteenth Century," in *Sixteenth Century Essays and Studies,* ed. C. S. Meyer (St. Louis: Foundation for Reformation Research, 1971), 2:47.

51. "The Shape of Reformed Piety," in Robin Maas and Gabriel O'Donnell, *Spiritual Traditions for the Contemporary Church* (Nashville: Abingdon Press, 1990), 215. See also Reid, "The Battle Hymns of the Lord," 2:36–54.

Chapter 7: Piety and the Believer

1. *Inst.* 3.6.2.
2. *Inst.* 3.6.3.
3. *Inst.* 3.7–8.
4. *Commentary* on 1 Timothy 4:7–8.
5. This section was first translated into English as *The Life and Conversation of a Christian Man* and has been reprinted often as *The Golden Booklet of the True Christian Life.*
6. See R. D. Loggie, "Chief Exercise of Faith: An Exposition of Calvin's Doctrine of Prayer," *Hartford Quarterly* 5 (1965): 65–81; H. W. Maurer, "An Examination of Form and Content in John Calvin's Prayers," Ph.D. diss., Edinburgh, 1960.
7. Due to space limitations, prayer is considered here in its personal dimension, but for Calvin prayer was also of vast importance in its communal aspect. See *John Calvin: Writings on Pastoral Piety*, ed. and trans. Elsie McKee (New York: Paulist Press, 2001), part 4, for a selection of individual and family prayers Calvin prepared as patterns for Genevan children, adults, and households, as well as a number of prayers from his sermons and biblical lectures. See also Thomas A. Lambert, "Preaching, Praying, and

Policing the Reform in Sixteenth Century Geneva," Ph.D. diss., University of Wisconsin, 1998, 393–480.

8. *Inst.* 3.20.3.

9. Ibid.

10. Charles Partee, "Prayer as the Practice of Predestination," in *Calvinus Servus Christi,* ed. Wilhelm H. Neuser (Budapest: Pressabteilung des Raday-Kollegiums, 1988), 254.

11. *Inst.* 3.20.4–16.

12. *Inst.* 3.20.11.

13. *Inst.* 3.20.34.

14. *Inst.* 3.20.14; Ronald S. Wallace, *Calvin's Doctrine of the Christian Life* (London: Oliver and Boyd, 1959), 276–79.

15. *Commentary* on Hebrews 7:26.

16. *Inst.* 3.20.17.

17. Lionel Greve, "Freedom and Discipline in the Theology of John Calvin, William Perkins, and John Wesley," Ph.D. diss., Hartford Seminary Foundation, 1975, 143–44. For how Calvin's emphasis on prayer impacted the Reformed tradition, see Diane Karay Tripp, "Daily Prayer in the Reformed Tradition: An Initial Survey," *Studia Liturgica* 21 (1991): 76–107, 190–219.

18. *Inst.* 3.3.1–2, 6, 18, 20.

19. *Inst.* 3.3.5, 9.

20. *Inst.* 3.3.3; Randall C. Gleason, *John Calvin and John Owen on Mortification: A Comparative Study in Reformed Spirituality* (New York: Peter Lang, 1995), 61.

21. *Inst.* 3.3.8–9.

22. John H. Leith, *John Calvin's Doctrine of the Christian Life* (Louisville: Westminster/John Knox Press, 1989), 70–74.

23. *Inst.* 3.7.1.

24. *Inst.* 3.7.2.

25. *Inst.* 3.7.4–5.

26. *Inst.* 3.7.7; Merwyn S. Johnson, "Calvin's Ethical Legacy," in *The Legacy of John Calvin,* ed. David Foxgrover (Grand Rapids: CRC, 2000), 74.

27. *Inst.* 3.7.8–10.

28. Richard C. Gamble, "Calvin and Sixteenth-Century Spirituality," in *Calvin Studies Society Papers,* 1995–1997, ed. David Foxgrover (Grand Rapids: CRC, 1998), 34–35.

29. *Inst.* 3.8.1–2.

30. *Inst.* 3.8.3–9.

31. *Inst.* 3.8.7–8.

32. *Inst.* 3.9.4.

33. *Inst.* 3.9.5.

34. Wallace, *Calvin's Doctrine of the Christian Life,* 170–95.

35. *Inst.* 3.9.3.

36. *Inst.* 3.10.

37. Greve, "Freedom and Discipline in the Theology of John Calvin," 20.

38. Leith, *John Calvin's Doctrine of the Christian Life,* 82–86.

39. Ford Lewis Battles, *The Piety of John Calvin* (Grand Rapids: Baker, 1978), 29.

40. I. John Hesselink, "Calvin, Theologian of Sweetness" (unpublished paper delivered as The Henry Meeter Center for Calvin Studies Spring Lecture, March 9, 2000), 10–16.

41. For Calvin on assurance, see Randall Zachman, *The Assurance of Faith: Conscience in the Theology of Martin Luther and John Calvin* (Minneapolis: Fortress Press, 1993); Joel R. Beeke, "Making Sense of Calvin's Paradoxes on Assurance of Faith," in *Calvin Studies Society Papers, 1995–1997,* ed. David Foxgrover (Grand Rapids: CRC, 1998), 13–30, and *The Quest for Full Assurance: The Legacy of Calvin and His Successors* (Edinburgh: the Banner of Truth Trust, 1999), 39–72.

42. *Inst.* 3.21.1.

43. In *Selected Works of Calvin,* ed. and trans. Henry Beveridge (Grand Rapids: Baker, 1983), 1.c. For piety in Calvin's own life, see Battles, *Piety of John Calvin,* 16–20.

44. Johnson, "Calvin's Ethical Legacy," 79–83.

45. See Erroll Hulse, "The Preacher and Piety," in *The Preacher and Preaching,* ed. Samuel T. Logan Jr. (Phillipsburg, N.J.: P&R, 1986), 71.

46. Hughes Oliphant Old, "What Is Reformed Spirituality? Played Over Again Lightly," in *Calvin Studies VII,* ed. J. H. Leith (Davidson, N.C.: n.p., 1994), 61.

Chapter 8: The Call to Cultivate Holiness

1. *The Marrow of Theology,* trans. and ed. John D. Eusden (1629; Boston: Pilgrim Press, 1968), 77.

2. Jerry Bridges, *The Pursuit of Holiness* (Colorado Springs: Navpress, 1978), 13–14.

3. This is apparent from the Dutch word for sanctification, *heiligmaking* (literally: "holy-making").

4. See Lawrence O. Richards, *Expository Dictionary of Bible Words* (Grand Rapids: Zondervan, 1985), 339–40.

5. See especially Rudolf Otto, *The Idea of the Holy*, trans. J. W. Harvey (London: Oxford University Press, 1946).

6. Stephen Charnock, *The Existence and Attributes of God* (reprint, Evansville, Ind.: Sovereign Grace, 1958), 449.

7. *The Works of the Rev. John Howe* (1848; reprint, Ligonier, Pa.: Soli Deo Gloria, 1990), 2:59.

8. *The Works of Jonathan Edwards* (1834; reprint, Edinburgh: Banner of Truth Trust, 1974), 1:101; see also R. C. Sproul, *The Holiness of God* (Wheaton, Ill.: Tyndale House, 1985).

9. R. A. Finlayson, *The Holiness of God* (Glasgow: Pickering and Inglis, 1955), 4.

10. *The Psalter*, 136.

11. Stephen C. Neill, *Christian Holiness* (Guildford, England: Lutterworth, 1960), 35.

12. Horatius Bonar, *God's Way of Holiness* (reprint, Pensacola, Fla.: Mt. Zion Publications, 1994), 16.

13. Quoted in Donald G. Bloesch, *Essentials of Evangelical Theology* (New York: Harper & Row, 1979), 2:31.

14. Quoted in John Blanchard, *Gathered Gold* (Welwyn, England: Evangelical Press, 1984), 144.

15. See George Bethune, *The Fruit of the Spirit* (1839; reprint, Swengel, Pa.: Reiner, 1972); W. E. Sangster, *The Pure in Heart: A Study of Christian Sanctity* (London: Epworth Press, 1954); John W. Sanderson, *The Fruit of the Spirit* (Grand Rapids: Zondervan, 1972); Jerry Bridges, *The Practice of Godliness* (Colorado Springs: Navpress, 1983); Roger Roberts, *Holiness: Every Christian's Calling* (Nashville: Broadman Press, 1985).

16. *Heidelberg Catechism*, Question 1 (the believer's status) and Question 114 (the believer's condition).

17. A. W. Pink, *The Doctrine of Sanctification* (Swengel, Pa.: Bible Truth Depot, 1955), 25.

18. Charnock, *The Existence and Attributes of God*, 453.

19. Aurelius Augustine, *Against Two Letters of the Pelagians*, 3.5.14, in *A Select Library of the Nicene and Post-Nicene Fathers*, first series, ed. P. Schaff (reprint, Grand Rapids: Eerdmans, 1982), 5:404.

20. John Calvin, *Institutes of the Christian Religion*, ed. John T. McNeill, trans. Ford Lewis Battles (Philadelphia: Westminster Press, 1960), 3.14.4ff.; see also Thomas Goodwin, *The Works of Thomas Goodwin*, ed. John C. Miller (Edinburgh: James Nichol, 1864), 6:220.

21. Quoted in John Blanchard, *More Gathered Gold* (Welwyn, England: Evangelical Press, 1986), 147.

22. Thomas Watson, *A Body of Divinity* (1856; reprint, Grand Rapids: Sovereign Grace Publishers, 1970), 173.

Chapter 9: How to Cultivate Holiness

1. Jerry Bridges, *The Practice of Godliness* (Colorado Springs: Navpress, 1983), 52.

2. Robert Bruce, *The Mystery of the Lord's Supper*, trans. and ed. Thomas F. Torrance (Richmond: John Knox Press, 1958), 82.

3. Quoted in Joel R. Beeke, *Holiness: God's Call to Sanctification* (Edinburgh: Banner of Truth Trust, 1994), 18–19.

4. D. Martyn Lloyd-Jones, *Romans: An Exposition of Chapter 6—The New Man* (Edinburgh: Banner of Truth Trust, 1972), 144.

5. Jerry Bridges, *The Pursuit of Holiness* (Colorado Springs: Navpress, 1978), 60.

6. James I. Packer, *Rediscovering Holiness* (Ann Arbor: Servant, 1992), 15.

7. See Jay Adams, *Godliness through Discipline* (Grand Rapids: Baker, 1973), 3.

8. Dietrich Bonhoeffer, *The Cost of Discipleship*, trans. R. H. Fuller (London: SCM Press, 1959).

9. Bridges, *Practice of Godliness*, 41–56.

10. "Baptism Form," in *The Psalter*, 126.

11. For Edwards's seventy resolutions to promote holiness made at nineteen years of age, see *The Works of Jonathan Edwards* (1834; reprint, Edinburgh: Banner of Truth Trust, 1974), 1:xx–xxii.

12. *Luther: Lectures on Romans*, trans. and ed. William Pauck (Philadelphia: Westminster Press, 1961), 189.

13. John Owen, *The Works of John Owen* (1851; reprint, London: Banner of Truth Trust, 1967), 6:20.

14. Quoted in I. D. E. Thomas, *The Golden Treasury of Puritan Quotations* (Chicago: Moody Press, 1975), 140.

15. See *Belgic Confession of Faith*, Article 28.

16. Thomas Watson, *The Mischief of Sin* (1671; reprint, Pittsburgh: Soli Deo Gloria, 1994); John Owen, *Temptation and Sin*, in *The Works of John Owen*, vol. 6; Jeremiah Burroughs, *The Evil of Evils; or The Exceeding Sinfulness of Sin* (1654; reprint, Pittsburgh: Soli Deo Gloria, 1992); Ralph Venning, *The Plague of Plagues* (1669; reprint, London: Banner of Truth Trust, 1965).

17. John Charles Ryle, *Holiness: Its Nature, Hindrances, Difficulties, and Roots* (reprint, Greensboro, N.C.: Homiletic Press, 1956); Octavius Winslow, *Personal Declension and Revival of Religion in the Soul* (1841;

reprint, London: Banner of Truth Trust, 1960); John Flavel, *Keeping the Heart*, in *The Works of John Flavel* (1820; reprint, London: Banner of Truth Trust, 1968), 5:417–507.

Chapter 10: Encouragements for Cultivating Holiness

1. Cited in John Blanchard, *Gathered Gold* (Welwyn, England: Evangelical Press, 1984), 144.

2. "The Spiritual and Carnal Man Compared and Contrasted; or, The Absolute Necessity and Excellency of Holiness," in *The Select Practical Works of Richard Baxter* (Glasgow: Blackie & Son, 1840), 115–291.

3. Cited in John Blanchard, *More Gathered Gold* (Welwyn, England: Evangelical Press, 1986), 149.

4. Thomas Watson, *A Body of Divinity* (1856: reprint, Grand Rapids: Sovereign Grace Publishers, 1970), 172.

5. John Owen, *The Works of John Owen* (1851; reprint, London: Banner of Truth Trust, 1967), 11:254ff; Joel R. Beeke, *Jehovah Shepherding His Sheep* (Grand Rapids: Reformation Heritage Books, 1997), 186–88.

6. B. B. Warfield, *Perfectionism* (Phillipsburg, N.J.: P&R, 1958), 100.

7. See Walter Marshall, *The Gospel Mystery of Sanctification* (reprint, Grand Rapids: Reformation Heritage Books, 2000), 220–21.

8. J. C. Ryle, *Holiness* (reprint, Greensboro, N.C.: Homiletic Press, 1956), 27.

9. Joel R. Beeke, *Assurance of Faith: Calvin, English Puritanism, and the Dutch Second Reformation* (New York: Peter Lang, 1991), 160ff.; see also the *Westminster Confession*, chapter 18, and the *Canons of Dort*, Head 5, for an appreciation of the intertwining of holiness and assurance.

10. Horatius Bonar, *God's Way of Holiness* (reprint, Pensacola: Mt. Zion Publications, 1994), ch. 2.

11. Watson, *A Body of Divinity*, 167.

12. Ryle, *Holiness*, 62.

13. Leonard J. Coppes, *Are Five Points Enough? Ten Points of Calvinism* (Manassas, Va.: Reformation Educational Foundation, 1980), 94–96.

14. Hugh D. Morgan, *The Holiness of God and of His People* (Bridgend, Wales: Evangelical Press of Wales, 1979), 9.

15. Andrew Murray, *Humility: The Beauty of Holiness* (Old Tappan, N.J.: Revell, n.d), 40.

16. Quoted in I. D. E. Thomas, *The Golden Treasury of Puritan Quotations* (Chicago: Moody Press, 1975), 141.

Chapter 11: Obstacles to Cultivating Holiness

1. William S. Plumer, *Psalms* (1867; reprint, Edinburgh: Banner of Truth Trust, 1975), 557.

2. J. C. Ryle, *Holiness* (reprint, Greensboro, N. C.: Homiletic Press, 1956), 1–2.

3. John Brown, *Expository Discourses on 1 Peter* (1848; reprint, Edinburgh: Banner of Truth Trust, 1978), 1:106.

4. Ryle, *Holiness*, viii.

5. Sinclair Ferguson, "The Reformed View," in *Christian Spirituality: Five Views of Sanctification*, ed. Donald L. Alexander (Downers Grove, Ill.: InterVarsity Press, 1988), 64.

6. John Owen, *The Works of John Owen* (1851; reprint, London: Banner of Truth Trust, 1967), 6:79.

7. Cited in John Blanchard, *More Gathered Gold* (Welwyn, England: Evangelical Press, 1986), 152.

8. Ibid., 149.

9. Peter Toon, *Justification and Sanctification* (Westchester, Ill.: Crossway, 1983), 40.

10. Cited in Blanchard, *More Gathered Gold*, 148.

11. John Murray, *Redemption Accomplished and Applied* (Grand Rapids: Eerdmans, 1955), 184–85.

12. Kenneth Prior, *The Way of Holiness: A Study in Christian Growth* (Downers Grove, Ill.: InterVarsity Press, 1982), 42.

13. See G. C. Berkouwer, *Faith and Sanctification*, trans. John Vriend (Grand Rapids: Eerdmans, 1952), ch. 6.

14. John Stott, *The Baptism and Fullness of the Holy Spirit*, 2d ed. (Downers Grove, Ill.: InterVarsity Press, 1975), 50.

15. Samuel Rutherford, *The Trial and Triumph of Faith* (Edinburgh: William Collins, 1845), 403.

Chapter 12: The Joy of Cultivating Holiness

1. Cited in I. D. E. Thomas, *The Golden Treasury of Puritan Quotations* (Chicago: Moody Press, 1975), 140.

2. Quoted in John Blanchard, *More Gathered Gold* (Welwyn, England: Evangelical Press, 1986), 153.

3. John Owen, *The Works of John Owen* (1851; reprint, London: Banner of Truth Trust, 1967), 3:310.

4. "The Crown and Glory of Christianity: or Holiness, the Only Way to Happiness," in *The Works of Thomas Brooks* (1864; reprint, Edinburgh: Banner of Truth Trust, 1980), 4:103–50. I have summarized Brooks's marks.

His entire treatise on holiness (446 pages) is an invaluable classic, but has been strangely neglected in contemporary studies on holiness.

5. J. C. Ryle, *Holiness* (reprint, Greensboro, N.C.: Homiletic Press, 1956), 71–72.

6. John Blanchard, *Gathered Gold* (Welwyn, England: Evangelical Press, 1984), 146.

7. See G. C. Berkouwer, *Faith and Sanctification*, trans. John Vriend (Grand Rapids: Eerdmans, 1952), ch. 2.

8. *Inst.*, 3.2.8.

9. Cited in Blanchard, *Gathered Gold*, 146.

Chapter 13: Your Private Life

1. *The "I Wills"' of the Psalms* (1858; reprint, Edinburgh: Banner of Truth Trust, 1985), 100.

2. *Commentary on John*, 2:288.

3. Cf. Richard Baxter, *The Reformed Pastor* (Edinburgh: Banner of Truth Trust, 2001), 74–75.

4. Cf. John Flavel, *Keeping the Heart* (Morgan, Pa.: Soli Deo Gloria, 1998).

5. *The Psalter*, No. 236, stanza 2.

Chapter 14: Your Prayer Life

1. *The Christian Ministry* (1830; reprint, Edinburgh: Banner of Truth Trust, 2001), 148.

2. Quoted in ibid., 148n.

3. *Lectures to My Students* (London: Passmore and Alabaster, 1881), 41.

Chapter 15: Your Relationship with God

1. Cf. James Stalker, *The Preacher and His Models* (New York: A. C. Armstrong and Son, 1891), lecture 2.

2. Baxter, *The Reformed Pastor*, 72–73.

Chapter 16: Your Family

1. In John Brown, ed., *The Christian Pastor's Manual* (1826; reprint, Ligonier, Pa.: Soli Deo Gloria, 1991), 75.

Chapter 17: Your Fight against Pride

1. *Puritan Sermons 1659–1689, Being the Morning Exercises at Cripplegate* (Wheaton, Ill.: Richard Owen Roberts, 1981), 3:378.

2. *The Reformed Pastor* (New York: Robert Carter & Brothers, 1860), 212–26.

3. Quoted in Charles Bridges, *Christian Ministry* (1830; reprint, Banner of Truth Trust, 2001), 153.

4. Ibid., 152.

5. *God's Plot: Puritan Spirituality in Thomas Shepard's Cambridge,* ed. Michael McGiffert (Amherst: University of Massachusetts Press, 1994), 82ff.

6. Quoted in Bridges, *Christian Ministry,* 128.

7. *Puritan Sermons,* 3:390.

8. In John Brown, ed., *The Christian Pastor's Manual,* 66.

9. *Preaching and Preachers* (Grand Rapids: Zondervan, 1972), 256.

Chapter 18: Your Coping with Criticism

1. James Sparks, *Potshots at the Preacher* (Nashville: Abingdon, 1977), 9.

2. Andy Stanley, *Visioneering* (Sisters, Ore.: Multnomah, 1999), 141ff.

3. *Pastors under Pressure: Conflicts on the Outside, Conflicts Within* (Epsey, Surrey: Day One, 2001), 30.

4. "Does the Shoe Fit?" *Journal of Biblical Counseling,* Spring 2002, p. 4.

Chapter 19: Your Preaching

1. Andy Stanley, *Visioneering* (Sisters, Ore.: Multnomah, 1999), 149–59.

2. Douglas F. Kelly, *New Life in the Wasteland: 2 Corinthians on the Cost and Glory of Christian Ministry* (Ross-shire, England: Christian Focus, 2003), 135–47.

3. "An Encouragement to Ministers in Trial," *Founders Journal* 16 (Spring 1994): 11.

4. *Lectures to My Students* (London: Passmore and Alabaster, 1881), 179.

Chapter 19: Your Preaching

1. Baxter, *The Reformed Pastor,* 119–20.

2. Ibid., 95–96.

3. *The Works of Thomas Brooks* (Edinburgh: Banner of Truth Trust, 2001), 3:217–18.

4. Cf. C. H. Spurgeon, *The Soul Winner* (New Kensington, Pa.: Witaker House, 1995), 98–99.

Chapter 20: Your Shepherding

1. Joel R. Beeke, *Jehovah Shepherding His Sheep* (Grand Rapids: Reformation Heritage Books, 1999).

2. *An All-Round Ministry* (1900; reprint, Edinburgh: Banner of Truth Trust, 1994), 305.

3. Horatius Bonar, *Words to Winners of Souls* (Phillipsburg, N.J.: P&R, 1995), 34.

4. Ibid., p. 33.

5. *A Minister's Obstacles* (Westwood, N.J.: Revell, 1959), 37.

6. In John Brown, ed., *The Christian Pastor's Manual*, (1826; reprint, Ligonier, Pa.: Soli Deo Gloria, 1991), 76–77.

7. *The Art of Manfishing* (MacDill, Fla.: Tyndale, 1971), 33.

8. *Words to Winners of Souls*, 31–32.

Chapter 21: Your Persuasions to Overcome

1. Cited in Charles Bridges, *The Christian Ministry* (Edinburgh: Banner of Truth Trust, 2001), 19n.

2. Ibid., 23.

3. *An All-Round Ministry* (1900; reprint, Edinburgh: Banner of Truth Trust, 1994), 393–94.

INDEX OF SCRIPTURE

Joel R. Beeke (Ph.D., Westminster Theological Seminary) is president of Puritan Reformed Theological Seminary, where he also serves as professor of systematic theology and homiletics. He is pastor of Heritage Netherlands Reformed Congregation in Grand Rapids, Michigan, and editor of *Banner of Sovereign Grace Truth*. Beeke is the author of *Puritan Reformed Spirituality, The Quest for Full Assurance*, and *A Reader's Guide to Reformed Literature*, among others. He and his wife have three children.